M000115392

REMEMBERING THE

KENNEBUNKS

REMEMBERING THE
KENNEBUNKS

KATHLEEN OSTRANDER

Charleston   London

THE
History
PRESS

Published by The History Press
Charleston, SC 29403
www.historypress.net

Copyright © 2009 by Kathleen Ostrander
All rights reserved

Images are courtesy of the author unless otherwise noted.

First published 2009

Manufactured in the United States

ISBN 978.1.59629.707.4

Library of Congress CIP data applied for.

Notice: The information in this book is true and complete to the best of our knowledge. It is offered without guarantee on the part of the author or The History Press. The author and The History Press disclaim all liability in connection with the use of this book.

All rights reserved. No part of this book may be reproduced or transmitted in any form whatsoever without prior written permission from the publisher except in the case of brief quotations embodied in critical articles and reviews.

CONTENTS

Preface   7

The Baxter Bible   9
The House that Sank   11
The Furbish Twins   14
Buckskin Sam   16
Hidden in the Fireplace   18
The Way Way Shop   20
The Butland Homestead   22
Fought with John Paul Jones   24
Hometown Baseball Stars   27
Romance of the Sawdust   30
Fear in 1940   33
Elias Hutchins—The Old Sailor   36
The 27th Maine   39
Drakes Island   40
Sea Creatures of New England Waters   43
Old Bet   46
Roscoe Stephens and His Telescope   48
Scandinavian Influence   50
Days of Prohibition   53
Civil War Story   55
The Walker Diaries   59
Boon Island   61
The Witch's Grave   64
The KKK in Maine   66

CONTENTS

The Murder of Dr. Swett   69

Tragic Death of Lizzie Bourne   71

The Doc Snow Gang   73

The Cat Mill   75

The King's Marker   77

The Real Scarlet Letter   80

Keeping Up with Madelyn Marx   81

Nelson Wentworth   84

Robert Canney Sr.   87

The Loss of the *Thresher*   90

Two Mysteries in Eliot   92

The Alfred Jail   94

Twelve o'Clock High   96

Vision of Mars   99

Slavery in Maine   101

Witch Trot Land   103

William Barry   105

The Kennebunkport Playhouse   109

The Saco Drive-In Theatre   111

Captain James Fairfield   114

If Trees Could Talk   117

Labor Day Remembered   118

Our Native American History   120

Remedies and Afflictions   122

Odd Sayings and Their Origins   124

About the Author   127

PREFACE

Upon moving to Kennebunk in the early 1980s, I became fascinated with the early architecture that can still be seen here. I grew up with a love of history, thanks to my father, and I have always loved things pertaining to early America.

Knowing that York County, Maine, was part of the original Massachusetts Bay Colony, I became interested in learning as much as I could about its nearly four hundred years of history. I spent a lot of time researching old deeds and photographs. I would scour antique stores looking for old documents and newspapers and spent more time than normal reading microfilm at the library.

Eventually, I became involved with the Brick Store Museum of Kennebunk, which I liken to a community attic on a grand scale. It is a wonderful place and resource, filled with all kinds of tangible evidence of the area's past. There are photographs, ledgers, diaries, paintings, pieces of furniture and just about anything else one can imagine within its walls. For a number of years I was the assistant archivist, and I still remain involved there as much as time now allows me.

I was fortunate to become involved with the Kennebunk Free Library years ago as well and was allowed to catalogue a collection of photographs known as the Ken Joy Collection. Ken Joy was a history buff who once wrote a weekly column in the *York County Coast Star* newspaper. That column was called "Out of the Past" and featured stories of Kennebunk and York County.

I approached the editor of that paper myself a number of years ago and suggested a similar column. Dan King, the editor at that time, came up with the name "Paging Through History." For three years, I wrote a weekly history column in much the same format as Ken Joy had done decades earlier. In the process, I was able to indulge my own fascination with York County history.

As most authors do, Ken would make a mistake here and there, and true to fashion, so did I. The former Kennebunk town historian, Joyce Butler, offered that "these mistakes happen" and told me that "they are like stones in a field and every now and then we are bound to come across some." Keeping that in mind, although we lovers of history try to be as accurate as possible in relaying our stories, we admit that once in a while we get some bits wrong. On that note, I will apologize in advance if you stumble on something here in my latest book that is in error.

This book is a collection of a number of those stories I wrote for the newspaper. They have been tweaked and added to in some ways, and I hope that you find them as interesting as I have. The majority, I would have to say, relate to Kennebunk, but several are about the surrounding towns and people who once lived in them here in old York County, Maine.

THE BAXTER BIBLE

Durrell's Bridge spans the Kennebunk River between Kennebunk and Kennebunkport and was named for an early settler of the area, Phillip Durrell. In 1703, Indians attacked Phillip Durrell's family.

During the attack, Durrell's wife, two daughters, Rachel and Susan, and two sons were taken. According to Bradbury's *History of Kennebunkport*, the Indians carried their prisoners as far as Fryeburg, where Mrs. Durrell persuaded them to let her return with her infant, also named Phillip. One of the Indians carried the child for her to the stone fort at Saco, from which point she returned to her home. Her other son and daughters remained with the Indians and continued toward Canada. This son drowned while crossing a river. The two daughters made it to Canada, where they remained and eventually married.

About 1725, during what was known as Lovewell's War, the Indians were once again enticed by the French to capture British settlers and take them to Canada, where they would be sold to the French for a small sum. The French would then try to ransom them back to the settlers for an even larger sum.

The Durrell family was once more attacked in October 1725. Phillip had left his home with one of his sons in the morning, and upon his return prior to sunset, he found that the Indians had set his home on fire, stolen his clothing and other articles and kidnapped his family.

This time, his wife, his son Benjamin and his daughter Elizabeth Baxter, wife of John Baxter, were taken. Elizabeth was pregnant at the time. Also abducted was her twenty-month-old son, John. With them, the victims took a family Bible that had been brought to this country by Elizabeth's husband. The large Baxter Bible was printed in 1628 and was a family treasure.

Search parties were sent out but found no trace of the family. Colonel John Wheelright of Wells, in a letter to the lieutenant governor of Massachusetts, wrote that Durrell and search parties had "searched the woods and found no signs of any killed."

The following spring, Phillip Durrell again searched the woods after the winter snow had melted and found the remains of his family and the Bible.

The Baxter
Bible.

The tomahawk head found by Phillip Durrell.

At a conference with the Indians in Falmouth the following year, the Indians admitted to having killed Mrs. Durrell, her daughter Elizabeth and Elizabeth's twenty-month-old son. It was later revealed that during their march through the forest, the Indian chief Wahwa, fearing discovery due to the infant's cries, ordered that the child and its mother be killed. He then ordered that Mrs. Durrell also be killed (perhaps to prevent her from slowing their progress, as it was rumored that she was lame). It became legend that she died while clutching the Bible. Benjamin was carried to Canada, where he remained for two years. When he was returned to his family, it was said that he had been forever changed by the horrific event.

Later histories by Bourne and Remich give conflicting information with regard to which children were kidnapped and which survived each episode, but regardless of that, the Bible itself remains as a testament (no pun intended) to a frightful era in early American history.

The Bible, along with a stone tomahawk blade that Phillip Durrell recovered from the scene of the murders, is occasionally exhibited at the Brick Store Museum in Kennebunk. The Bible is on long-term loan from the family of Katherine Adams Brown. The tomahawk blade was a gift to the museum from the Mabel W. Kelley Estate in 1961.

THE HOUSE THAT SANK

Somewhere off the shores of Monhegan Island lies a colonial house whose windows open onto the ocean floor. It sits in sixty-five fathoms of water. That's six feet per fathom! It began its life in West Rockport, Maine, having been built sometime around the time of the Revolutionary War. It was known as the Old Wilson House and overlooked Mirror Lake and the Oyster River Pond. It was nestled in the same rugged terrain for close to two hundred years.

One winter in 1963, an ad appeared in *Down East* magazine that offered the Cape Cod–style home for sale, but it would have to be moved. The Rockland Water Company owned the land on which it sat but, realizing the house's age, hoped to have it moved rather than destroyed. The company understood a concept that many can't grasp in this day and age—that preservation is also progress.

Many inquired and thought better of the idea once they realized that it might be impossible to move over land due to various bridges in the

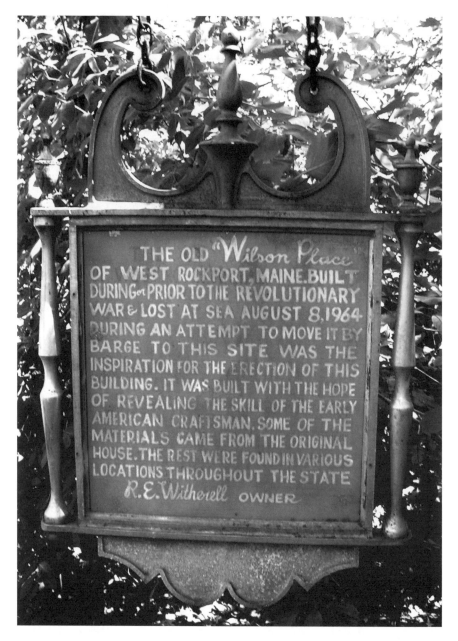

A sign in Kennebunkport that marks the property where the antique Cape was meant to be placed, had it survived the journey.

area. The house was one and a half stories tall, with two rooms up and five rooms down. It measured a tidy twenty-four by thirty feet and had an ell that measured ten by fourteen feet. It had a massive central chimney, twelve by twelve feet, which dominated much of the floor plan. The original bricks and beehive oven were also intact. The Camden Historical Society verified from old deeds that it was occupied as early as 1783. The society suspected but could not prove that it had been built about ten years prior to that.

Richard Witherall and his wife happened upon the ad and began thinking that this house might be exactly the kind of home that they would love to have on their land in Kennebunkport. Richard owned Witherall's Radio and Television Service in Saco at the time, and he and his wife also owned a small parcel of land on what is known as Cleaves Cove. They began researching the project and realized quickly that the house could not be moved over land, but what about over sea? They decided to buy the house. After more than six months of planning, they had lined up a company to transport the house from its original site and another company to sail it by barge to Kennebunkport, where it would be towed ashore. They acquired insurance from a company that was not named in the papers of the day. It was referred to only as a "rather sporting insurance company."

On the day the house was to start its journey, mover James Merry attached cables and sleds to the building to haul it up and out of the rugged area it was in. Only the main portion of the house was to be moved over sea. The ell, being smaller, would go at a later time by flatbed truck. It took Merry six hours to move the house six hundred feet. While in progress, the building detached from its cables and slipped back ten to fifteen feet. This happened six times! It was as though the house didn't want to leave the land on which it was built. Once it was finally raised onto Merry's flatbed truck, he started toward Rockland Harbor. During this leg of the trip, he broke an axle and accidentally tore up one large tree by its roots. Again, it seemed that the house wanted to remain where it had always been.

The entire flatbed truck and house were loaded on a barge in Rockland, and the wheels of the truck were blocked with timbers. Cables also tied the building down. A tugboat skippered by Captain Clark and his crew of four was to tow the barge to Kennebunkport.

The weather looked favorable when Clark and his crew began their departure at high tide that evening. By 1:15 a.m., they were close to Monhegan when reports came over the radio warning of severe weather. There was no moon, and the sea began to roll violently in a gale that seemed to come out of nowhere. The crew of the tugboat could hardly stand, and one man was sent crashing into a cabin window. He was not hurt, but the window was smashed. Immense tension could be felt by all.

At 2:15 a.m. the captain called for a check of the barge. It was hard to balance on the moving deck, but finally a spotlight was brought to shine on the barge. The house was gone. "The spotlight was swung out to shine across the sea. Barely visible astern, was the old house on its way down," the glass in its windows reflecting the spotlight eerily back at the crew.

The Witheralls were notified about 3:45 a.m., and after learning that no one had been injured, their disappointment began to register. Insurance eventually covered the loss, and the Witheralls used timber from parts of the ell that had not been shipped over sea to build a home at Cleaves Cove.

If you're biking or driving out Ocean Avenue this summer, take a turn on Halcyon Lane. There is a small replica Cape Cod–style home with a sign that pays tribute to the Old Wilson Home.

THE FURBISH TWINS

If you're interested in local stories, just have a yard sale. I am a person who hates having yard sales. I dread setting them up and having the front lawn look like a scene from the old television series *Sanford and Sons*. Unfortunately, stuff has a way of piling up. So once a year I box up all my "stuff" and drag it outside for a yard sale.

This year I met a man from the Wildes District area of Kennebunkport who told me how his father, when he took corn to the gristmill, would bring him to town on the back of the wagon when he was a small child. While the corn was being ground, his father took the horse to have it shod. The man told me that Wildes District was called "Monkey Town," but he didn't explain why.

Another couple was looking for old bottles and canning jars. This couple shared with me their knowledge of coyotes and black bears.

This year's best story was told to me by a relative of the Furbish twins. Kent Berdeen and his wife told me many things about the twins, who were his great aunts. Their names were Ethel and Edith Furbish. They were born in 1888 and lived in the house now located at 14 Sea Road in Kennebunk, built by their father, George.

George forbade his daughters to marry unless they were married on the same day. Although both girls were engaged at various times in their lives, they never did marry.

Both twins had blue eyes. They dressed the same and grew old together in the home where they grew up. The house was never centrally heated, and although there was indoor plumbing, the cat box was placed in the shower stall for their many cats. They saved everything—even cat food tins, after they had washed them out.

Through most of their lives, they had a loving relationship, but Kent said that as they grew older, they had times when they truly seemed to hate each other. He recalled that one of the twins would take naps in the barn, and if she heard her sister climbing up the loft ladder, she would slam the loft door down on her head. He said that at one point one sister

The Furbish twins.

had a stroke, and she lay on the floor a couple of days before the other realized she wasn't faking.

Eventually, the twins entered the Saco River Health Care Center in Biddeford, where they lived out the remainder of their days. Edith, born five minutes before Ethel, outlived her sister.

When the home on Sea Road was cleaned out, thousands of dollars were found hidden throughout the house. That money went toward the twins' care at the health center.

Great stories! I wonder what I'll learn at next year's yard sale.

BUCKSKIN SAM

In 1900, a man sat down at the urging of his friends and began to write the story of his unusual life. For years he had been telling remarkable tales of travel and adventure. At the age of sixty-two, he put his story together in a

Buckskin Sam.

book that he published himself. He titled it *The Life of Buckskin Sam*. It is a strange and remarkable tale, 185 pages in length.

Buckskin Sam, as he was known later in life, was born Samuel H. Noble in Kennebunk, Maine, in 1838. His father was a local innkeeper who died when Sam was only three years old. After his father's death, his mother moved the family to New Sharon, Maine, to live with her parents. At the age of six, Sam was "bound out" to work and live with a man in Fayette, Maine.

I find it hard to imagine a boy so young being sent away to live and work with a man who was a total stranger. Perhaps in those days it was common. The wages he earned were sent home to support his family. This arrangement lasted three years. Sam then went to live with an uncle and returned home to his mother in 1849. That summer he began school.

What is interesting about Sam's writing is that he describes things in great detail. He includes descriptions of how his school looked, where children were required to sit and the temperament of the teacher. Unfortunately, he disliked school and got into a great deal of trouble. The schoolmaster would punish him by beating him with alder branches. According to Sam, after one such beating, the schoolmaster "commenced the battle cry of freedom upon my poor back, but I did not forget to laugh."

After only one season of school, Sam decided to leave home. He was only eleven years old at the time. It was the middle of February when he packed a bundle of clothes and his gun and walked to Thomaston, Maine, a distance of twenty-five miles. He headed down to the docks and found several ships in port. He discovered one schooner that had his mother's name, the *Elizabeth*, so he immediately signed on with the captain of the vessel as a "chief cook and bottle washer".

Thus began his life of adventures. He sailed around the world to different ports on various ships. He alternated between making a decent living and being desperately poor. He stayed in towns all over the world in sailors' boarding homes with folks who would steal his shoes and clothes to sell if he wasn't watchful.

While traveling, he also saw things that most people his age only dreamed of—some wondrous and some frightening. Like most sailors of the day, he would remain in one town only long enough to find work on the next ship that needed a crew. In his book, he describes seeing giant sea turtles, whales, dolphins and sharks. This was quite a departure in education from what he had experienced in the one-room schoolhouse at home.

In Buenos Aires, he struck a deal with a farmer to tend his sheep. While out on the plains, he was captured by local Indians and held hostage for six years. From that time, he was known as "Buckskin Sam." During his captivity, he learned many survival techniques, which, to the dismay of the reader, he offers way too much gory detail describing. I could have gotten away quite happily without reading his graphic descriptions of how the Indians prepared their meat.

When Sam finally escaped from the Indians, he headed back to the port in Buenos Aires and immediately took work on a ship that was headed to England. In Liverpool, he was impressed into service by the British navy, becoming a captive again, of a different sort!

After years of travel and fighting in Russia, China and East India, he finally made his way back to America, which, to his surprise, was embroiled in a civil war. Of course, he signed up for this as well. He claims to have fought with Custer and to have been at the surrender of General Lee at Appomattox Court House.

I would certainly say that Sam's life was one less ordinary. He returned to Kennebunk after his ramblings but soon became weary of idleness. Off he went again, claiming that he would undoubtedly "continue to rove until old age shall incapacitate me or death shall claim me as his."

In 1886, Sam was sent to jail for a five-year sentence for causing trouble in Lawrence, Massachusetts. I am not sure if he died there or where he finally lived out his days or even where he is buried. Those details, in comparison to the amazing details of his life, seem inconsequential.

HIDDEN IN THE FIREPLACE

I'm told that years ago there was a gentleman who did odd jobs around town. He would clean basements, attics and the like. His favorite type of home in which to offer his services needed only to meet the criterion of being very, very old, preferably colonial. Apparently, what was known to him, but not to those who hired him, was a colonial tradition that involved a particular hiding place for valuables.

In ancient chimneys, some early families would hide a metal or wooden box in which they could safely store their valuables. Some boxes were hidden in the arches that supported the chimneys; some were tucked up behind the mantel. After all, who would go sorting through all that soot and ash? As families moved or ancestors passed away, the box was often forgotten. Grandpa would sometimes forget to tell anyone where he hid the family

A colonial shoe found hidden behind the mantel of the Ebenezer Rice house in Kennebunk during renovations.

jewels. Apparently, the fellow found quite a bit of treasure this way, mostly in the form of jewelry or coins.

Another odd tradition of colonial times involved placing a shoe in the stonework of a chimney before building the fireplace surround and adding the mantel. Many colonial shoes have been found by stone masons hired to re-point or rebuild fireplaces in York County. This summer while working on a fireplace in Kennebunkport, Richard Irons, a restoration mason from Limerick, came across an early shoe tucked in a crevice within the stonework. According to various legends, it was a practice to place a shoe for good luck somewhere in the structure when building a house.

Once thought to be a fairly uncommon practice restricted to Northern Virginia and Pennsylvania, more and more incidences of this tradition are being discovered throughout each of the colonial states. Just why the tradition originated is unclear. While searching the Internet, I found very little to explain the tradition or point to its origins. One site suggested that the tradition was meant to scare away evil spirits or witches that might view fireplaces as "openings" through which to enter the home. The shoe as a good luck symbol was meant to warn them off. Another notion suggests that the shoes may have been intended to act as a kind of bait. Witches would be lured into the trap by the smell of the shoe, and once there, they would be unable to escape since, as everyone knows, witches are unable to travel backward.

In England, concealing shoes is a well-known folk custom and is so common throughout the country that the Northampton Museum has set up a Concealed Shoes Index to record all the occurrences. The museum receives an average of one find a month but says that hundreds of finds every year may well be simply thrown out by builders. In Britain, as many as fifty shoes date from before 1600. The numbers rise to more than five hundred in the nineteenth century, and then the finds trail off. Shoes have also been found under floorboards and hidden behind plaster walls.

If you have come across an old shoe during a restoration project, perhaps you should document it and let your local historical society know about it. It is a wonderful example of a lost tradition. And for those of you living in a colonial-era home, perhaps more than a shoe will turn up!

THE WAY WAY SHOP

There are two hundred homes listed on the National Register of Historic Places website for York County, Maine. One of them is a tiny shop located in Saco on Route 112. Although its doors are now closed for good, it was known for years and years as the Way Way Shop.

The Way Way Shop was given its name because at the time it was built, it was way, way out of town! Route 112 was known as the Buxton Road. When the shop was built, it was a gas station catering to a fairly new invention called the automobile. It was also a general store. The station was built by a man named Eugene Cousens and his son who hauled stone and gravel to the site and mixed the concrete by hand.

They sold everything in the early days, from men's work clothes to groceries and tools. Eugene's daughter Peggy began working there when she was fourteen years old, selling sodas. Many of the original tin advertising signs remain hanging on the walls, where they have been since the beginning. Also on the walls are old photos of Peggy and her father at the shop when she was only a child. Both are shown standing in front of the old Tydol gas pumps.

In later years, when I began taking my daughters there, it was known as a candy shop with one of the last penny candy counters left in the state of Maine. Candies that many of us remember from our own youths could still be found there. Each type of candy was identified by a hand-lettered sign. To name a few, there were Red Hot Dollars, Razzles, Flying Saucers, Mary

Peggy Cousens and her niece, Catherine Cousens, man the candy counter at the Way Way Shop in Saco.

The Way Way Shop in Saco, Maine.

Janes and bubble gum shaped like cigars. Prices ranged from ten cents up to fifty-five cents. Some novelty items were ninety-nine cents.

By the 1980s, the town of Saco seemed closer and closer to the shop, having been built up substantially over the years. As a result, the Way Way Shop wasn't that far away anymore, and more folks came to it each year to absorb the olden days feel of the place. They also came to allow their own kids to experience the joy of looking through a glass countertop at a giant assortment of candy.

Just prior to their closing, I stopped in with my daughter and her friends after a soccer game at the nearby Saco Middle School. There was Peggy in her eighties and her niece, Catherine Cousens, in her seventies, ready to greet us and help the kids choose their candy. I asked them how they felt about closing after all those years. They seemed generally ready and anxious to no longer have to be open seven days a week. They seemed ready, too, to not have to stand on their feet for eight hours each day. I asked them what their new plans included, and with a quick wink and a laugh Peggy responded, "To have a life!"

I came away wondering how many children had stood at their counter over the years and how many would recall the memory. The Way Way Shop will remain on the National Register, and for now the ladies have no plans to sell the building. The original shop cases and tin advertising signs will stay right where they have always been—hopefully forever, if only in our mind's eye.

THE BUTLAND HOMESTEAD

On the Sea Road in Kennebunk there is a small home that has stood for over two hundred New England winters. This post-and-beam-constructed home has been lovingly restored by Greg and Sue Church. Originally, this home stood closer to the Mousam River and was owned by the Butland family. Two Butland cemeteries can be seen in the woods behind the home, one close by and the other, older one, nearer to the river.

A large center chimney with its beehive oven has been recently uncovered, as well as early feathered-wood paneling. The hand-hewn beams show the telltale marks of an ancient adz. Throughout renovation, the Churches have found hand-cut nails, vintage wallpaper and early pine boards, some measuring over sixteen inches wide.

Although the exact date of construction has not been determined, historian William Barry wrote that this was in fact the home of William

The Butland homestead on Sea Road, Kennebunk.

Butland, his father and, prior to that, a man named John Look. Early deeds reference all three men, but little is known of John Look. There is a wealth of information in local biographical sketches about William Butland.

The Butland family lived through some of the worst years of the earliest settlement of New England. They experienced the Indian Wars and lived to tell of them. They also built the first ship on the Mousam River. Over twelve ships would be built over the years at their shipyard on the Mousam's banks.

Edward Bourne, a local historian, told a number of stories about William Butland in his book *History of Wells and Kennebunk*. One recounts that as a child, while William's parents were away at church, the house was visited by Indians. William, who was nine years old at the time, could see one of the Indians peering through a small hole in the door. So he took a spindle from his mother's workbasket and stabbed the Indian in the eye with it. Luckily, the Indians fled. Bourne actually learned many of the stories from William Butland himself, who lived until 1828.

Another story related that Butland, as a grown man, went to look for his cows one day. He could hear the bell of one cow getting farther and farther away from the settlement. He followed the sound for a good distance before he realized that the Indians had the bell and were trying to set a trap for him. He had gone too far to go back to his home for safety. In a moment of insight, he climbed inside the hollow of a fallen tree. Soon the Indians surrounded the spot, looking for him. The Indians began to beat on the trunk but were fearful to enter either end as they were not sure which way William's gun was pointing. Soon, family members who were worried at his long absence came to find him and frightened the Indians away.

After surviving such difficult times, William's death came here in his own home. In 1828, at the age of ninety-five, while standing near the open hearth, he accidentally had his cane knocked out from under him by a child in the house, and he fell into the burning embers of the fireplace. The burns he received resulted in his death only a few days later.

Luckily, thanks to historians like Bourne, William's stories remain, and thanks to folks like Sue and Greg Church, so does his home.

FOUGHT WITH JOHN PAUL JONES

Kennebunk resident Henry Tilton told me an interesting story the other day. Apparently, Henry and his companions have spent a great deal of time clearing and maintaining some of the old cemeteries in Arundel over the years. One of the graves they came across is situated in a small family plot off Route 111, near the Arundel border.

The fellow buried there led a life less ordinary. His name was John Burbank, and although he grew up miles from the ocean, he chose a life on the open seas. I cannot find any reference indicating what drew him to work on sailing ships, but during the Revolutionary War he sailed with none other than Patriot John Paul Jones.

John Paul Jones, whom George Washington considered to be the naval hero of the Revolutionary War, was captain of various ships. In September 1779, Jones was captain of a ship called the *Bonhomme Richard*, which came under attack by the enemy ships *Serapis* and *Countess of Scarborough*. The *Bonhomme Richard* was originally armed for protection against pirates in far eastern waters and carried its guns (twenty-eight twelve-pounders) on one deck, with six lighter pieces (six-pounders) on the poop deck and forecastle. Jones had ports cut in the gun room on the deck below, where he mounted six eighteen-pound guns. Jones named the ship the *Bonhomme Richard* in honor of Benjamin Franklin, who used the name Poor Richard as a pen name for his almanacs and who, at the time, was the American ambassador to France.

John Burbank of Lyman was the master at arms on this vessel. It was during this famous battle between the *Bonhomme Richard*, the *Serapis* and *Countess of Scarborough* that John Paul Jones became legendary for saying, "I have not yet begun to fight!" In researching this story, I learned that he in fact never said those words. The *Bonhomme Richard* was heavily damaged in this battle, which was known as one of the fiercest in naval history. At one point, the chief carpenter cried out to John Burbank and fellow shipmate Henry Gardiner that the ship was sinking. Gardiner rushed to the bridge to haul down the American flag to surrender, which he would have done if the flagstaff has not already been carried away during the battle. The captain of the *Serapis* called to Jones, asking if he was ready to give quarter. In his own record of the event, Jones claimed that he replied, "*Je ne songe point à me*

Life as a sailor on the high seas.

rendre, mais je suis determiné à vous faire demander quartier." Translated from the original record in the Library of Congress, this reads, "That point didn't occur to me, but I am determined to make you ask for quarter." In 1825, a biographer loosely translated the record to create the legendary phrase that we know today.

In the same report in the Library of Congress, Jones recounts the actions of John Burbank in less than charitable terms. He claims that

> *the idea that the* Bonhomme Richard *was going to sink had so deranged the Master at Arms mind by excessive fear that he opened the hatches and, despite my repeated orders to the contrary, let out all of the prisoners we had, numbering 100. At the time of outfitting, the commissioner had refused to provide iron chains for the prisoners, and this mental derangement of the Master at Arms might have become fatal, if I had not taken advantage of the prisoners' fear and put them to work at the pumps where they displayed surprising zeal, appearing to have forgotten that they were prisoners and that nothing could prevent their leaving the* Bonhomme Richard *to board the* Serapis, *as it was entirely in their power to put an end to the fight by killing me or throwing me overboard.*

As I read this account, I have to think that Burbank, still in his twenties at the time, acted admirably because he believed that the prisoners would drown if the ship sank. In his mind, he most likely believed that he was saving their lives.

The entire battle lasted four hours. The hold of the *Bonhomme Richard* was more than half filled with water when the enemy surrendered. Through the night, the pumps were manned to keep the ship afloat. The next morning, everyone onboard the *Bonhomme Richard* was transported to other ships, which had finally arrived to aid it. Once everyone had been removed from the ship, the pumps were no longer manned and the *Bonhomme* sank to the bottom of the ocean.

I was unable to find out what became of John Burbank following the battle. Perhaps he was one of forty-five men who went on to fight with John Paul Jones in subsequent naval battles. Perhaps he was one of those who were "clapped in irons" and sent back to America.

In the end, Burbank died here in York County at the age of ninety-one on October 3, 1843. His stone bears the following inscription: "A Revolutionary soldier in the navy engagement under John Paul Jones." He is buried next to his wife, Anna, who died in 1810.

HOMETOWN BASEBALL STARS

In old towns across America, streets and monuments have routinely been named after earlier residents who lived there. Bridges and buildings bear the name of the original builders, and parks and playgrounds often get named for prominent people. Some historic markers commemorate war veterans, authors or politicians. But mostly, our neighborhood homes only bear silent witness to those who have lived within their walls, famous or otherwise.

Out in the Alewive section of Kennebunk stands a house whose walls could certainly tell a tale or two about the famous ballplayers who lived there. One was John W. Coombs, better known as "Colby Jack Coombs," and the other was his nephew, Bobby Coombs, who also played Major League Baseball.

To look at early photos of the old farm and the people who lived there, one would never guess that he was looking at anyone famous. Colby Jack can be seen in hunting clothes or with his car, at a barbeque or standing on the front porch with his father. But anyone who really knows baseball knows that

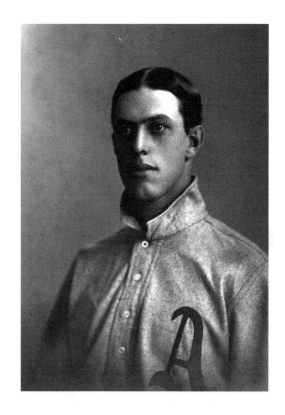

A young Jack Coombs in a Philadelphia Athletics uniform. *Courtesy of the Wentworth family.*

Above: Gathered with family members on the front porch of his Alewive home, Jack Coombs is on the right, in the back row, standing next to his father. *Courtesy of the Wentworth family.*

Left: Colby Jack Coombs. *Courtesy of the Wentworth family.*

Raymond "Bobby" Coombs.
Courtesy of the Wentworth family.

Colby Jack was indeed famous!

Jack W. Coombs took his nickname from the college he attended. He graduated from Colby College in Waterville, Maine. The baseball field at this college is named Coombs Field after Jack. Coombs was recruited right from college into the Major Leagues as a pitcher for the legendary Connie Mack and the Philadelphia Athletics. His accomplishments include beating the Chicago Cubs in the World Series three times. Another amazing record was set when he pitched a twenty-four-inning victory over Boston. His career also included pitching for the Brooklyn Dodgers, after which he went on to coach baseball at Duke University. He coached at Duke for twenty-four years. Duke University named its baseball field after Coombs as well.

During the off-season, he would return to the farm in Alewive, where his parents lived, and spent his time hunting, fishing and being with his relatives. One relative was his nephew Raymond, who was known as "Bobby" Coombs. Colby Jack must have had quite an influence on his nephew, who also went on to become a Major League baseball player. Bobby graduated from

Kennebunk High School and went on to Duke University, where his uncle was coaching. From Duke, he was recruited by the Philadelphia Athletics and later went on to play with the New York Giants. Following his career with the Giants, he went on to coach at Williams College, which incidentally named its baseball field Coombs Field after him.

During their years in baseball, these Alewive boys played with and against some of the greatest names in the sport. Colby Jack played with Chief Bender and Eddie Plank and pitched against Ty Cobb and Cy Young. Young Bobby pitched against none other than Babe Ruth.

I believe that all homes have stories to tell, but this one in Alewive seems to have more than its share. It was finally sold out of the family in 1986.

ROMANCE OF THE SAWDUST

There is a road over in Wells Branch named Chick Crossing Road. When I was new to the area, I pondered the name, not knowing how it came about. I envisioned cute baby ducks prone to crossing that road as a hazard to be mindful of. Only much later I learned that this road was named after a man with the last name of Chick who allowed the railroad to cross his land in this part of Wells back in the mid-1800s.

This section of Wells is one that still has many antique Cape-style houses. Many were originally built by Littlefields. On Chick Crossing Road, there is also a sawmill standing in a meadow. I have driven by it several times and wondered how old it is, so I went in search of that answer by contacting the owners, Carl and Joan Goodwin.

Instead of just a story about a sawmill, I found a story about a way of life. I found a story of family heritage and Yankee ingenuity that I'd like to share with you.

Carl Goodwin and his wife, Joan (Nadeau), were married over fifty years ago. Carl grew up on the farm where they still live. As a boy, he attended the school up the road that has since been converted into a fire station. His father grew up on the same farm, as did his father before him and his father before him and so on. Nine generations can trace their roots to this very same property, and many of these ancestors are buried in the family cemetery just beyond the sawmill.

The original building was a Cape that, in 1906, was taken apart to create

Carl Goodwin's sawmill on Chicks Crossing Road in Wells.

a larger home. The original ell and barn remain.

Carl's father, also named Carl (but without a middle initial), ran a chicken farm on the property for many years before he came across a man in Kennebunk Lower Village named Frank Emery who had purchased a secondhand sawmill made by the Lane Manufacturing Co. Frank sold the disassembled mill to Carl Sr., who up until that point had never run or operated a sawmill.

Carl Sr. then got together with a millwright in Berwick named Tuttle who agreed to help him set up the mill. A neighbor named Waldo Chick built the building to house the mill. Now the only thing missing was power. The year was 1940. A friend of Carl's named Joe Polito drove a taxi in Kennebunk. The car he used as a taxi was a 1927 "straight 8" Packard. The car was old but the engine was strong. Together they took the car to "Harold O'Brien's garage" and had the engine removed. They mounted it on skids and took it out to the mill, where Carl and Frank Emery turned it into the power source.

The mill became operational, but Carl soon realized that the sound of the mill was too loud and unnerving. So he decided to hire a sawyer to run the saw. A commercial lot was set up and Carl concentrated on using his own timber lots as the wood supply. Any size board could be cut, including special orders. The mill ran on weekends for close to thirteen years. Carl never again returned to chicken farming.

Sadly, Carl Sr. died in 1953, leaving his widow, Clara, alone on the farm. Carl Jr., then living in New Jersey with Joan, decided to move back home. He also decided to take on the task of making a living with the sawmill. Although he had never operated the mill before, he put his engineering degree to work to master the task. He read all the books he could find about operating a sawmill, including one with a goofy title called *Romance of the Sawdust*. He used a chart that his father had made and hung in the mill to try to figure out how the different settings were used to adjust the size of the cut made. It was a frustrating learning process, until a friend named Edwin Morse offered a simple sawyer's saying, "Inches are ahead and quarters are back." Within this saying was the key to setting "the works of the mill," and Carl was able to get the mill up and running in no time.

He ran a successful business with the aid of his wife until the mid-1980s. He made spare parts from all sorts of things when no spare parts could be found for purchase. He used the engine of his mother's 1936 Dodge to run a machine called an "edger," which was used to cut the bark from the edge cuts of logs.

As for most farmers his age, Yankee ingenuity came into play many times. There is a saying where I come from that if something is broken, someone like Carl "can put it together with no more than a bit of spit and bailing twine if needs be."

The mill still runs occasionally. It was used most recently to cut boards for a horse barn and a two-car garage for one of Carl and Joan's children, as well as for some beams cut specifically to be exposed in their new home.

I am always in awe of folks like the Goodwins. Carl's father went away for a short while to pursue his college education at Tufts University and Wentworth Institute and then returned to the family farm with his wife, Clara, a Colby graduate. Then his son, Carl, went away to pursue his college degree in engineering from the University of Maine and, for a short while, took a job in New Jersey, but when the time arose, he too came home to the farm he had always loved.

Carl and Joan raised three girls and three boys on the farm and have now retired. They have ten grandchildren and winter in Florida each year. Five of their children live fairly close to the old farm in Wells, and one lives near them in Florida during the winter months.

They shared old memories, old family photos and laughter with me, and I couldn't help but come away believing that corny but sweet slogan to be true—"Maine, the Way Life Should Be!"

FEAR IN 1940

The summer of 1940 will be remembered in pre–World War II days as one of anxiety, in which patriotism was questioned and tempers got incredibly out of hand on more than one occasion.

Throughout York County that summer, rumors circulated that various people belonging to a certain religious sect were approaching people in their homes and suggesting that their children not salute the American flag in school. The intention of the sect was most likely to suggest that God be more revered than government. But in the tense years leading up to World War II, the sect was accused of being pro-Nazi. In Sanford, two members of the Jehovah's Witness sect were severely beaten when they refused to salute the American flag.

In Kennebunk, there was a building on Summer Street just two buildings away from Depot Street called Kingdom Hall. This was known as the local headquarters of the Jehovah's Witnesses. Following the incident in Sanford, as rumors ran rampant and tempers ran high, the members of the Kennebunk sect barricaded themselves in their hall on Summer Street, fearing that they, too, would be attacked. The sect's leaders, Joseph Leathers and Edwin Bobb, had complained that the windows of their hall had been smashed by rocks,

Carroll S. Madsen and Joseph Leathers. *Courtesy of the Associated Press.*

6 JAILED IN MOB DISORDERS

CARROLL S. MADSEN (LEFT) AND JOSEPH

LEATHERS, MEMBERS OF A RELIGIOUS SECT

IDENTIFIED BY STATE POLICE AS JEHOVAH'S

WITNESSES, ARE SHOWN ABOVE IN THE SANFORD,

ME., JAIL AFTER A MOB OF ABOUT 2,000 PER-

SONS SET FIRE TO THE SECT'S HEADQUARTERS

AT KENNEBUNK JUNE 9. TWO KENNEBUNK MEN

IN THE MOB WERE WOUNDED BY GUNSHOT PELLETS

FIRED, POLICE SAID, FROM THE BUILDING.

MADSEN, LEATHERS AND FOUR OTHER MEMBERS OF

THE SECT WERE CHARGED WITH ASSAULT WITH

INTENT TO KILL.

ASSOCIATED PRESS PHOTO
6/10/40. BXJPH1216PED
EAST ABC (BX LIST 0..)

An Associated Press description of the mob activity.

and they had appealed to Governor Burrows for protection.

Exactly what took place about midnight on June 9, 1940, will never be known, except by those who were there, but the night left two men wounded by gunfire, one of whom would have to have his leg amputated. At first, the local radio stations circulated wild stories of the night's events, and city papers released greatly exaggerated stories. They claimed that twenty-five hundred townspeople of Kennebunk, armed with torches, marched down Summer Street and that the "mob" ransacked and set fire to the Kingdom

Hall after news had been circulated that two townsmen had been shot by members of the Jehovah's Witness sect.

At trial, events unfolded to reveal that on several nights leading up to the night of June 9, several cars had been seen cruising slowly by the sect's headquarters on Summer Street, windows of the hall had been smashed and members of the sect believed they would be targeted by violence. About 2:30 a.m. on the ninth, a car with four young men in it stopped in front of the hall. The men, Kennebunk residents, said that they were merely stopping to change drivers, although one witness claimed that she had actually seen them park their car, cross the street to the hall and return when the firing was heard. One of the men was said to have been limping. The four men then got in their car and left.

The injured men were taken to Dr. Stimpson's for treatment of gunshot wounds and then sent to Trull Hospital in Biddeford. One of the men had been shot through the left thigh and in several places in the lower part of the leg, resulting in the need for amputation. State policemen who responded to the shooting arrested five members of the Jehovah's Witness organization and took three women into protective custody. All of them were placed in the Kennebunk jail until a crowd of about twenty-five gathered in front of the jail door. Fearing that violence might be attempted, the state police took the men to the county jail in Alfred and put the three women on a bus to Portland.

The following day, a large group of Kennebunk citizens allegedly ransacked the Kingdom Hall and set fire to it. Two men were taken into custody and charged with arson. On the Monday morning following the events, the five members of the Jehovah's Witness organization who had been arrested were brought from Alfred to Kennebunk and pleaded not guilty to assault with a dangerous weapon with intent to kill. Bail was set by Judge Bourne at $10,000 each, and the defendants, unable to furnish securities, were taken back to Alfred.

Eventually, trials were held for both the shootings and the arson, and of the five members of the Jehovah's Witness sect initially arrested, four were acquitted and one was sentenced to state prison. Edwin Bobb of Kennebunk, a leading member of the Jehovah's Witness organization, was sentenced to two and a half years in prison for assaulting Dwight Robinson with intent to kill. Those accused of arson were found not guilty. The Kingdom Hall was eventually torn down.

ELIAS HUTCHINS—THE OLD SAILOR

A few years ago, I picked up a small paperback booklet at Harding's Bookshop in Wells. This pamphlet was a reprint of a story originally published in 1853. It was called *The Old Sailor: A Thrilling Narrative of the Life and Adventures of Elias Hutchins during 40 Years on the Ocean, Related by Himself*.

I was intrigued to read the story of Elias because I had heard that this very same man lay buried in an unmarked grave in the cemetery once used as the Town Poor Farm of Kennebunk.

At the time of this story, related by Elias himself, he had apparently fallen on hard times and was living at the poor farm. "Wishing to free himself from public charge," he engaged the help of a friend named William Bryant to write the story of his life. Elias believed that many would find his trials remarkable and this would provide him with an income.

Within the forty-nine pages of the booklet, Hutchins describes his early life as less than remarkable, admitting that he, from infancy, was nursed on the lap of poverty and reared in the school of adversity and privation. His father drowned before his birth, and his mother was left to support the family on her own. Placing her future hopes on Elias to support the family, she was discouraged to find that Elias yearned to take to the sea and travel the world. She tried unsuccessfully to dissuade him.

In 1797, at just thirteen years old, Elias gained his mother's consent to sign on with Captain John Perkins as a cook aboard the brig *Morning Star*. He was to be paid five dollars a month. In exchange for her consent, he promised her that it would be his first and last voyage.

When he returned home three months later, he had decided that a life on the sea was his destiny and broke his promise to his mother. He signed on with the ship *Aurora* within three weeks. As time went on, he made a point of passing on the majority of his wages to his mother and by doing so, gained her eventual support.

At fifteen years old, he enlisted in the U.S. Navy in Norfolk, Virginia. It was 1799, and he found life in the navy to be intolerable. Officers with whips in hand stood over the crew, ready to beat anyone who disobeyed their commands. When his term of one year was over, he gladly accepted his discharge and went ashore once again in Norfolk.

His pay, which amounted to about seventy dollars, was quickly spent, and he found himself unemployed and homeless. Regretfully, he again enlisted in the navy for another year of cruelty. Upon discharge in Washington, D.C., he

THE

OLD SAILOR:

A THRILLING NARRATIVE

—OF THE—

LIFE AND ADVENTURES OF

ELIAS HUTCHINS,

DURING 40 YEARS ON THE OCEAN.----Related by Himself.

WRITTEN BY WILLIAM M. BRYANT

BIDDEFORD
PRINTED AT THE EASTERN JOURNAL OFFICE
1853.

The cover of the book by Elias Hutchins.

The Kennebunk Poor Farm that once stood on the Cat Mousam Road. *Courtesy of the Brick Store Museum.*

began his journey home, taking various vessels and a stage until he reached New York, where he again ran out of money. He again turned to the sea.

It seemed that Hutchins had found his pattern in life—constantly taking employment on various ships only to spend all of his wages ashore. His travels took him to see the world. He went to Curacao, Tangiers, Majorca and the Straits of Gibraltar, to name a few places. During his travels, he experienced hurricanes, shipwrecks and starvation.

His greatest adventure came shortly after a ship he was on was captured by the British in 1803. He was forced to serve in the British naval service aboard the ship *Hydra* of forty-six guns. For two years, he sailed with the *Hydra* in its campaign against the French and Spanish. In October 1805, the *Hydra* was one of many ships to join Lord Nelson's fleet in the Battle of Trafalgar.

In 1816, at age thirty-three, when he finally made his way home, he found that his mother had married a man named Frances Varney. During Hutchins's long absence, his mother had believed him to be dead. When he was finally able to see his mother again, she had a very hard time believing that he was really her son.

Hutchins continued working on the sea until his health prevented it. Having no savings, he found himself at the mercy of the town coffers. His book never did gain him financial independence, and sadly, he eventually died at the poorhouse and was buried at its cemetery. No stone marks his grave or those of any of the other thirty or so unfortunates who died there.

THE 27TH MAINE

John J. Pullen, author of the book *A Shower of Stars*, died in 2003. He was born in Amity, Maine, and was well known for his books about the Civil War. *A Shower of Stars* was written about soldiers from York County, Maine. It was written as an investigation into the reason 864 members of the 27th Maine Infantry were awarded the prestigious Medal of Honor and whether they deserved it.

In September 1862, the 27th Maine Regiment of Infantry Volunteers was mustered out of Portland, Maine. All were York County men, from towns such as Kittery, Biddeford, Kennebunk, Kennebunkport, Wells and Dayton, given a bounty for enlisting in the Union army for a period of nine months' service. They were sent by train to defend the capital at Washington, D.C.

A reunion of the members of the 27th Maine at the Arundel Grange Hall in 1910. At least six of the men can be seen wearing their Medals of Honor. *Courtesy of the Brick Store Museum.*

During their enlistment, twenty-two died of disease while on the picket line, due to inclement weather. The regiment fought in no battles.

In June 1863, with only days left in their enlistment, the members of the regiment were preparing to return home. At this same time, however, General Lee and the Confederate army were headed toward Gettysburg. All of the defenses that could be spared were sent to General Meade to confront Lee at Gettysburg. Unfortunately, this left Washington, D.C., vulnerable to attack should Lee turn toward the city.

President Lincoln and Secretary of War Edwin Stanton appealed to the two remaining regiments currently defending Washington to extend their services until the emergency was over. The 25th Regiment of Maine Volunteers flatly refused and went home.

Colonel Mark Wentworth of Kittery persuaded 309 of his men to stay. This was less than half of the regiment, but Stanton was overjoyed and directed that every man who had opted to stay receive the Medal of Honor. The 309 men stayed in service an additional four days and returned home, never engaging in a single battle.

Due to a bureaucratic mix-up, and because an accurate list of the 309 men who stayed was never verified, all 864 men of the 27th Maine were awarded the Medal of Honor. Medals were sent to Colonel Wentworth in Kittery in January 1865 following the war. Wentworth believed that not one of his men really deserved a Medal of Honor but decided to try to follow Stanton's orders by giving them to the 309 men who had remained with him in Washington. He stored the rest of the medals in his barn. Eventually, they disappeared.

In 1916, the U.S. government tried unsuccessfully to recall the medals. As of 2009, over four hundred medals are still unaccounted for. The government made it a criminal offense to own (unless in a museum) or sell one of these medals. In a 1910 reunion photo of the 27th Maine Regiment taken at the Grange Hall in Arundel, at least six veterans can be seen wearing their medals.

DRAKES ISLAND

It was Mabel Kelly's birthday on the morning of August 5, 1915. The previous night there had been a frightening storm. She awoke expecting to hear "Happy Birthday" being sung to her, but instead she heard someone yelling about a shipwreck on the beach.

An early postcard, circa 1910, shows cottages on Drakes Island.

Hastily, she ran to the beach, where she found fellow cottage neighbors Mr. and Mrs. Clogston. The three of them started toward the surf. It was still rainy and foggy from the previous night's gale. Eventually, they came upon what appeared to be part of a ship's cabin resting on the sand. It measured eighteen by twenty-five feet and its sides were crushed. A man's body was lashed to the cabin door, with only his hands showing above the sand. They turned around with a shudder to find the wreckers coming up the beach to exhume the body. Later that day, they learned that the cabin was part of the ship *Mary E. Pennell* and that the captain, Edwin Frye, from Machias, was the unfortunate man lashed to the cabin door.

This is but one of the many stories told by Mabel Kelly in her book *History of Drakes Island*, which she published in 1949.

Drakes Island is said to have received its name from a man named Thomas Drake who lived on a small island in Casco Bay. Drake sailed the Maine coast from Yarmouth to Wells, establishing trading posts with the local Indians. It is not known whether Drake ever actually lived on Drakes Island. The name has been used on maps for over three hundred years. Early settlers of the island included Captain Joseph Hill, John Wakefield, John Cross and Stephen Batson. From 1675 to 1730, during the French and Indian Wars, the island was deserted.

When the Boston Tea Party took place in 1773, a family named Donnel was living in York, Maine. Unwisely, Captain Donnel brought a cargo of tea into York Harbor. Donnel, a supposed Loyalist, was not held in high regard as a result. It is not known if it was by choice or pressure that the Donnel family later moved to Drakes Island.

While the Revolutionary War was in progress, little attention was paid to how the Donnels came into possession of the land. The home they built still stands and for many years was known as the Eaton farm, after those who later came to occupy it in 1883. The Donnel family is buried in a small cemetery behind the farm.

Joseph Eaton sold the first parcel of land on the island to John Lord in 1895 and Lord built the first summer cottage there in 1897. More lots were soon sold by Eaton, and soon the early cottages of Littlefield, Gillis, Adams, Clogston, Spooner, Caroll and Woodman were built.

Mabel Kelly's father met Mr. Eaton and bought a lot for his cottage on the waterfront near the Wadleighs and Peases. He called his cottage Samoset. This cottage was later renamed Colcord. Six more cottages were built. Then, for a number of years, according to Mabel Kelly, the colony did not increase much. She likened the island to a large family. There were no electric lights—only bonfires and lantern glow.

There were a few Grand Army of the Republic (GAR) men living and working in the colony. Among them was Moses Bragdon, who was known to wear his broad-brimmed GAR hat while working around the island. Mabel said that Moses always thought in terms of the Civil War, and although he never won a Purple Heart, he highly prized a bullet that had passed through his body during battle, nearly killing him.

Another GAR man was Mr. Spooner, who built the cottage known as Morning Side. These men were veterans of the Civil War, as was Joseph Eaton, who held a two-day encampment on his farm for his comrades. These men had been a part of the Company I, 1st Maine Regiment of Cavalry. During the evening hours, fellow cottagers would join Eaton at his campfire to hear the men tell tales about their war years.

As the colony grew and more cottages were built, a form of self-government was adopted, called the Drakes Island Improvement Society. A store was eventually built by John Hill, and fairs were held annually on the lawns. Highly decorated tables and novelties attracted many people from off the island as well. Buckboard parties from as far away as York would come to the annual fairs.

On certain Sundays, the island ministers conducted services outdoors in a grove of trees. Artists such as Charles Woodbury and Abbott Graves came to paint on the island. Mabel described Woodbury as a painter who always sat facing west, while Graves always sat facing east.

In 1908, the first car arrived on Drakes Island when a friend of the Kellys came for a visit in his red Stanley Steamer. Within a few years, Mabel's father purchased his first car, which was steered by a long lever like a tiller. At that time, to obtain a license, one had simply to drive one hundred miles. Her father drove ninety of those miles on his way home from Boston with the car. The car salesman came with him.

Drakes Island today, although much more populated, is still a quaint retreat, with many of its early cottages still standing.

SEA CREATURES OF NEW ENGLAND WATERS

Part of the fun of reading through old newspaper archives is finding stories of mythical creatures. In the mid-nineteenth century, giant squid, sixty-foot sea serpents and even mermaids were common sightings related in local papers.

New England had its share of sea serpent sightings. Eyewitness accounts give descriptions of huge snake-like creatures similar to modern descriptions of the Loch Ness Monster. Popular news magazines of the mid-1800s, printed elaborate illustrations of giant octopi attacking sailing ships.

One news magazine of 1842 called *Vox Populi* printed in-depth articles on the existence of mermaids, with illustrations of one mermaid said to have been regularly exhibited in Boston. The *Vox Populi*, printed in Lowell, Massachusetts, claimed that the creature was about three feet long, with a lower body like a perfectly formed fish and an upper body more nearly approaching a human form, with a pair of well-formed breasts, arms and hands. The creature was further described to be bald on the top of its head, but the sides of its head were covered with hair that extended down its neck in ringlets. The cheeks, eyes and lips were said to resemble those of a human. Other descriptions from local papers claimed that the face was like that of a young female, with fine, light blue eyes.

In Boston, Gloucester, Newburyport and Penobscot Bay, fisherman and sailors told of giant sea snakes. In 1830, the *Harper's New Monthly* magazine

An early newspaper depiction of a giant sea snake.

told of various sightings of a serpent-like creature that could travel at a rate of a mile or so per minute and claimed that its head was like a rattlesnake's but as big as a horse's. The magazine went on to report that the body appeared rough and scaly, measuring between forty and sixty feet long, and its tongue was two feet in length.

During that same year, fishermen in Wells and Kennebunk spotted the same serpent on several occasions in late June while fishing near the mouth of the Kennebunk River.

> *Two of the men were so much alarmed that they went below deck. The third however, Mr. Gooch, a man whose statements can be relied on, remained on deck and returned the glances of the serpent for a considerable length of time.*

Mr. Gooch claimed that the creature came within six feet of the boat, raised its head from the water and looked directly in the boat, so remaining

An early newspaper depiction of a mermaid.

for several minutes. Daniel Remich's *History of Kennebunk* related this same story and reported that Mr. Gooch said that he could have easily struck the serpent with his oar but was willing to let it alone if the serpent chose not to bother him.

I think about these fantastic old tales and wonder if in another one hundred years or so, people will be able to look back on our time, with its alien encounters and UFO sightings, and poke a bit of fun at us too.

45

OLD BET

My travels took me over to Alfred, Maine, via Route 4 one weekend. I had read years ago about one of the first elephants to arrive in America and heard, too, that the poor creature met its demise in Alfred. So, with the aid of the Internet, I went in search of a memorial marker.

In the summer of 1804, an African elephant named Betty arrived in Boston and became a local exhibit there. One of those who came to see Betty was a farmer and cattle merchant named Hachaliah Bailey, who found her to be the most magnificent creature he had ever laid eyes on. Four years later, Bailey was shocked to discover that Betty was being sold at a cattle market. He bought her and took her back to his hometown of Somers, New York, where he hoped he could use her to help on the farm, and perhaps he could also charge his neighbors for a peek. He renamed her Old Bet. Within a few years, Bailey gave up farming and spent the majority of his time as a showman. He exhibited a variety of animals, including a horse, several pigs, a trained dog and Old Bet, which was obviously the main attraction. A document in the Somers Historical Society shows that Bailey also sold shares in Old Bet to two other partners for $1,200 each.

An early postcard of an elephant.

Within a few years, the partners decided to take the show on the road and began a traveling exhibition. In 1816, they led Old Bet on a tour of New England. They arrived in York County during the summer of that year and visited many towns, including Wells and Kennebunk.

An interesting point of reference is that this exhibit came on the heels of the War of 1812. The years leading up to the war and during the war were desperate times of poverty and despair. By 1816, a year after the Treaty of Ghent ended the war, Old Bet came to York County. It must have been a magnificent event in people's lives and a spectacle of unparalleled proportions!

Upon leaving Kennebunk, the group headed to Alfred. It traveled on foot during the evening to prevent people from viewing the creature for free. It is not clear exactly what day Old Bet reached Alfred. Some reports say that it was July 24; others say it was the twenty-sixth, and some say the twenty-seventh. What is recorded is that the group stopped in a farmer's field just off what is now Route 4 in Alfred. Just before daylight, as they readied to walk Old Bet into town, she was shot dead in her tracks. The farmer who killed her was described as a religious zealot who did not believe that someone should be making a living by enticing poor people to pay to see the elephant.

Some believe that the shooting occurred on the twenty-seventh and that the farmer was enraged because they were planning to exhibit her on a Sunday. The farmer's name is not given in any of the pages I read on the subject, nor was there any mention of punishment.

Old Bet's death did not stop her from going on exhibition, however. Nine months later, it was advertised that her owners had stuffed her, and for the next four years, her remains toured New England.

Bailey went on to purchase two more elephants and also built a hotel in his hometown of Somers to commemorate the creature responsible for his fortune. It was named the Elephant Hotel and still stands to this day. He also erected a tall statue on the Somers village green that is decorated with the figure of an elephant.

In 1821, the American Museum in New York announced that it had purchased Old Bet to be on permanent display. I am not sure if she is still there. However, if you take a drive out to Alfred some day, be sure to take a left on Route 4. Just up the road on your left, before the York County Jail and sheriff's office, you will see a stone monument on the side of the road. Here, at the intersection with Swetts Bridge Road, the marker (dates and spellings questionable) reads:

July 24ᵗʰ 1816
Sight of slaying of elephant exhibited by Hackaliah Bailey and George Brown Company of Somers, NY

July 24ᵗʰ 1963 Thomas H.J. Scott, Doner of site Sanford-Alfred Historical Society.
Eugene Chariot; Chairman: Circus Fans of America.

ROSCOE STEPHENS AND HIS TELESCOPE

When I was a kid, my family spent a lot of time camping. We traveled to the Amish country near Gettysburg, Pennsylvania, and to Freeport, Maine, to name a few places. We watched mankind first walk on the moon from a campground in Hershey, Pennsylvania.

By the time I became a teenager, we no longer went on camping trips because, well, let's face it, not many teenagers go camping with their parents. Many years have passed since those days of camping, but I still remember most of the places we went.

On one trip to Shelburne, Vermont, we stayed in a large, open-field campground. While we were there, the nights were crystal clear, and my dad and I would lie on the grass and look up at the stars for what seemed like hours. We could spot constellations and satellites and watch shooting stars. I recall that it was mesmerizing to see.

In Kennebunk, there was a man who felt that same way about the night sky, so much so that he built himself a giant telescope to view it with. His name was Roscoe Stephens, and he originally came from Sumner, Maine. He, too, had loved watching stars as a child. This hobby grew into a passion. At ten years old, his father gave him a book called *Fourteen Weeks of Astronomy*. With the help of the book, he calculated the movements of the planets through the seasons. He set up a planetarium in his attic and spent his nights watching the heavens. His dad later gave him a spy glass. Although not a telescope, it did improve his observations.

Roscoe moved to Kennebunk shortly after his marriage. Through the years, he continued his study of astronomy. In 1933, he became interested in building his own telescope. He sent away for what was called a "Blank." He also ordered the tools and abrasives to grind the Blank into a lens. His first lens was too small, and he found it unsatisfactory, so he ordered another. It

Roscoe Stephens with his telescope. *Courtesy of the Brick Store Museum.*

took him six months to grind and polish the twelve-and-a-half-inch lens to perfection. He then ordered a nine-foot tube, made in a Portland foundry, to house the lens. He purchased a motor and a prism and began the work of teaching himself how to put together a telescope. He even had to create the gears to operate it.

When the instrument was done, Roscoe began to focus on creating a building to house it in. He planned and built a small building in his backyard on Barnard Lane. It had an easily removable roof that used a clever system of ropes and pulleys to open it.

He later combined his interest in astronomy with his interest in photography and was able to create stunning images of the moon and other planets using his telescope. He published these images in some of the popular magazines of the day.

Roscoe requested that his telescope be donated to a local college upon his death. In 1949, the telescope and ingenious observatory were donated to Bates College. His telescope now sits in the Stephens Observatory, named in his honor, on the roof of the Carnegie Science Building at the college. His legacy serves as a powerful learning tool for other students and lovers of astronomy.

SCANDINAVIAN INFLUENCE

In the 1890s, a group of immigrants arrived in Maine from the south of Norway. They were in search of a better way of life. Among the first to arrive in Kennebunk was a man named Samuel Tvedt. Sam soon recruited other family members and friends from Norway to join him.

His brother, Antoinne, came with his wife and began working in the local factory in town known as the Leatheroid Company. This company was located on Water Street and was responsible for the manufacture of a variety of products, including leatheroid-bound trunks and shipping boxes. Antoinne worked making roving cans, which were used in the woolen mills throughout New England. Roving cans were tall fiber canisters used to hold the long strands, or "rovings," of wool that were fed into looms to make cloth.

He was very successful at his job and built his family a new home on Winter Street in Kennebunk in 1893. His brother, Sam, held various jobs in town but was best remembered as a preacher of sorts. In the book *Kennebunk in the Nineties and Biographical Sketches*, authors Edward Bourne and Hartley Lord claim that Sam took up religion and once a week would come down to the square to preach:

> *Dressed in a long black coat, bareheaded, with hair flowing to his shoulders, bible in hand, he would take his place by the old town pump and launch into loud sermon, which due to the traffic noises and the fact that his English was not too perfect, was probably heard only by himself.*

Antoinne bought a building on Hall Street to be used as a church for the growing number of Scandinavian immigrants in town. Here his brother, Sam, would preach. The stained-glass windows can still be seen on what is now a private home.

Sam Tvedt, standing with his Bible. The man seated may be his brother, Antoinne. *Courtesy of the Brick Store Museum.*

Antoinne is indirectly responsible for my interest in local history. My husband and I bought our first home in Kennebunk, which turned out to be the house on Winter Street that Antoinne built in 1893. We lived at 4 Winter Street for eleven years. While there, some odd coincidences led me to investigate the deeds and vital records of the Tvedt family. This, in turn, piqued my interest in other homes in town.

The first unusual thing that occurred happened within the first six months of purchase. While exploring in the barn, I found the name Tvedt written on several walls in chalk or white paint. Next, I stumbled on a loose floorboard, which I removed to reveal a secret hiding place from long ago. In that small chamber beneath the barn floor, I found a time capsule of sorts.

There, on top of blown-in insulation, were two figurines—one of Pokey and one of Gumby. After removing them, I dug farther and discovered the wing of a model airplane of World War II vintage. Below that, I found a

The Antoinne Tvedt family posing in front of their home at 4 Winter Street in Kennebunk. *Courtesy of the Brick Store Museum.*

long-handled soap strainer. Even farther down, I discovered a paper fan with a beautiful lithograph of a lady in a canoe. It was an advertising fan from the defunct Acme Theatre, which at the time I had never heard of. Lastly, at the very bottom was a small, two-inch news clipping with words underlined in pen. This newspaper seemed to be neatly cut and of more recent vintage than any of the other items.

As I began to read it, a chill went up my spine. The article was about some sort of reunion. The article was referring to two "Syracuse boys living on Ostrander Avenue." The words Syracuse and Ostrander had been underlined. It was bizarre to find a newspaper article in a hiding spot of a barn with both my last name and the name of a town I grew up near underlined. If my name was more common, I suppose it wouldn't have unnerved me as much as it did. Were we meant to live there?

Another odd coincidence occurred later. After a couple of months, we began to remove the wallpaper in our bedroom to prepare the walls for painting. There were five layers of wallpaper over the old horsehair plaster. It was a tedious job. As we removed it, we realized that we could see extremely large letters written on the wall beneath the paper. After a number of days at the task, all of the letters were exposed. They spelled "Mark," which just happened to be my husband's name.

After eleven terrific years there, we decided to move. We didn't mention to the new owner that during the time we lived there, we had added some of our own clues for new generations to uncover. The walls in every room may someday be removed in future remodeling attempts, and there on the studs we left our own messages and dates in pencil. Under the flooring of one bedroom, we left a time capsule of our own in the year 2000. Lastly, in one bedroom, we concealed a giant mural that I painted on the wall for my daughter with a second layer of drywall to protect it.

I believe that every house needs a bit of a mystery!

DAYS OF PROHIBITION

My grandmother was a flapper. Photos of her with a perfect "question mark curl" and elegant clothes were always favorites among us grandchildren. I remember asking her once about Prohibition, as she was in her twenties during its heyday. She recalled going to a favorite speakeasy with my

Shown in this photo from left to right are Deputy Sheriffs Smith and Murphy, Sheriff Irving and Deputy Sheriffs Cullihan and Jones with a confiscated shipment of liquor in 1914.

grandfather and having to know the correct knock on the door followed by a password to gain entrance.

Maine was the first state to pass a prohibition law. That first law, in 1851, prohibited the manufacture and sale of "spiritous or intoxicating liquors" not intended for medical or mechanical purposes. Twelve more states adopted such laws by 1855.

Enforcing these laws was never an easy task. Here in Kennebunk in the early 1900s, the job fell to Sheriff Frank Irving and his men. During that decade, the newspapers were often filled with exciting tales of the sheriff and his men engaged in daring chases of rumrunners. Some chases were successful and some were not.

In June 1914, a rum car was captured at midnight in Wells. The car contained twenty-one wooden kegs, containing about eighty-three gallons of whiskey and twenty gallons of rum. It was related in the local papers the next day that Sheriff Irving and his officers drove over to the iron bridge in Wells and then took up a position under the bridge, with their car placed sideways across the road.

"It was a long wait and just before midnight the party heard a familiar sound of an auto coming down the road. All four men got ready for business." As the oncoming car reached the bridge, the officers pointed a powerful searchlight on the vehicle. The men in the car slammed the vehicle into reverse and attempted to back up. Just as the car had almost gotten itself turned around, the sheriff and his men were upon it. The two men in the car jumped out and began to run for the woods. Deputy Ernest Jones and his party fired four shots at the men, but they continued to run and succeeded in getting away.

The captured car with the load of contraband goods was driven to Kennebunk and placed in Larrabee's garage. Leon Herman of Portland came forward the following day and turned himself in. He pleaded guilty before Justice Harold H. Bourne and paid a fine of $100.00 and costs, amounting to $124.67. He was then released.

The Eighteenth Amendment, which prohibited "the manufacture, sale, or transportation of intoxicating liquors within, the importation thereof into, or the exportation thereof from the United States," was passed in January 1919 but was repealed by the Twenty-first Amendment in 1933.

Deputy Ernest Jones went on to become sheriff and later in life ran a candy store on Main Street in Kennebunk.

CIVIL WAR STORY

In the opening scene of the movie *Cold Mountain*, Union soldiers tunnel under a Confederate fort and succeed in blowing up much of it. Interestingly enough, this scene was actually played out on the real battlefield of the Civil War, and Horace H. Burbank was there.

I recently read Burbank's Civil War diary and pored over a scrapbook about his life that is part of the Brick Store Museum archives in Kennebunk, Maine. Burbank left us a remarkable testimony to his service in the Civil War and a vivid account of his life as a prisoner of war.

Burbank, born in Limerick, Maine, in 1837, enlisted in the Union army in 1862 and was mustered out as part of the 27th Maine Infantry. This unit

The Medal of Honor awarded to Horace Burbank.

Horace Burbank. *Courtesy of the Brick Store Museum.*

spent its term near Washington, D.C., for nine months but never fought in any battles. When the regiment's term of nine months was up, all but 350 or so men left for home. Burbank and others elected to remain to defend the capital for an additional four days. For this, they were awarded (questionably) the Medal of Honor. Burbank's medal is part of the Brick Store Museum collection. It is an odd feeling to hold the actual medal in your hands and realize the history behind it.

When Horace returned home, he continued his studies at Bowdoin and was admitted to the bar on January 13, 1864. In his diary, he wrote, "Near the close of this year, after Christmas, I left the law school for home, having another attack of army fever." A month and a half later, in March 1864, he reenlisted and found that "Captain Seth E. Bryant of Kennebunk is my Captain and a goodly number of the 27th Maine boys are also in the 32nd." The 32nd Maine Volunteers was the new regiment he'd joined, out of which he was mustered as a first lieutenant.

In April of that year, his regiment joined the 9th Corps under General Ambrose Burnside. Unlike his first experience with army life, this time he fought in many battles. On May 12, after the battle of Spotsylvania, Burbank wrote:

> *This morning at 4 o'clock work was begun along our whole line and at 5 our regiment found itself under a calling fire of shell and musketry, chiefly the latter. Thus we lay for 8 hours, sometimes more, sometimes less hot, on our faces or elbows as prudence dictated. We lost in killed and wounded, about 50. Lieut. Gurney fell dead three feet in my rear. It was a hard sight to visit the division hospital and see so many poor fellows mangled and marked in ways inconceivable.*

Burbank fought at Cold Harbor on June 3, commenting that the "carnage of the rebels was dreadful." On June 7, he became a captain of Company K. The units marched each day and encountered enemy fire routinely. On one day alone, one hundred horses were killed and "36 men were found in a pile, buried and half buried."

On June 16, having crossed the James River by pontoon bridge, the Army of the Potomac, as it was then called, began a series of operations outside the city of Petersburg, Virginia, one of which became famous as the Battle of the Crater. As in the movie *Cold Mountain*, the Union soldiers, using handbarrows made out of cracker boxes, began excavating eighteen thousand cubic feet of earth in an effort to tunnel under the Confederate fort known as Elliot's Salient, which contained 256 officers and men of the 18th and 22nd South Carolina.

The engraved back of Horace Burbank's medal.

At 4:45 a.m. on July 30,

> *a heavy roar, as if from the bowels of the earth, belched forth, and the occupants of that fort, all unconscious of the cause of their sudden awakening, started heavenward. Earth, stones, timbers, arms, legs, guns unlimbered and bodies un-limbed, amid clouds of dust and smoke, ascended in fearful confusion and havoc. It was a spectacle never to be forgotten.*

Unfortunately, due to poor command from their generals that day, Burbank and others became prisoners of war and were marched behind enemy lines, on their way passing Generals Lee, Beauregard and Mahone. "Circumstances did not conduce to making personal acquaintance," Burbank wrote. Eventually, they arrived at Danville Prison.

Burbank's account of prison life was detailed and appalling. Poor nutrition and improper sanitation, accompanied by lack of proper protection from the elements, eventually led to his confinement in a Confederate hospital, where, when his strength returned, he and eighteen others hid in the attic, undetected for two days, and eventually escaped under the cover of darkness to join General Sherman's army two months prior to the close of the Civil War.

When Burbank returned home, he moved to Saco, Maine, married a Kennebunk girl named Elizabeth Thompson, who was the daughter of sea captain Nathaniel Lord Thompson, and began practicing law. He remained a successful lawyer until his death in January 1905.

Burbank's chronicle of the past is a fascinating read to both those interested in Civil War history and those who are not familiar with that era. The graphic explanation of his life in Danville Prison to me is a testimony to the strength of the human spirit.

THE WALKER DIARIES

While digging into local history, I realized that Kennebunk is luckier than most towns in that it has a remarkable reference tool. At the Kennebunk Free Library on Main Street, Kennebunk, there is a set of diaries that were kept by a man named Andrew Walker. Walker, a local shopkeeper, kept his diary faithfully and daily for forty-five years of his life, beginning in 1852. Many diaries of this era were mere recordings of the weather and crops. Andrew's were detailed and colorful accounts of local life in his hometown.

Andrew's father came to what was known as Arundel, Maine, in the mid-1730s. He was a saddle maker. Andrew was one of eleven children. Andrew's mother was named Susanna Merrill and was also of Arundel. Andrew was born in October 1808. He was a student in the New Hampshire Literary and Biblical Institute during 1832 and 1833. Following his training there, he became a teacher for a brief period of time.

In 1835, he and his brother Palmer opened a mercantile business in Kennebunk. They ran this store together until 1840, when Palmer turned the business entirely over to Andrew. Andrew continued to run the business until 1888.

In 1857, Andrew married Harriet Purrington of Bowdoinham, Maine. Their only child, Lucy, died at the age of twenty-four from an unknown illness. Through the years, Andrew served as the director of the Ocean National Bank and was a town clerk and a town treasurer.

Andrew Walker.

What he is most remembered for is his diary, which he began at the age of forty-two. His first entry, dated January 1, 1851, gave the following explanation of his intent:

> *I Andrew Walker, propose to write a short diary in this book of such events in this quiet village and vicinity as come to my knowledge. By the term events, I include whatever may be suggested to my mind at the time of writing, whether private or public in nature, my own thoughts or the thoughts of others. In short, whatever may come uppermost that I shall try to express. How long the diary may continue, remains to be seen.*

His writings filled eleven volumes. He diligently wrote each day, even when some days he had nothing to offer of news. On some days, he would simply write that there was nothing of import to record. Most entries were more remarkable. His diaries spanned the Civil War years, and as town clerk, he recorded the names of the soldiers drafted from Kennebunk, their families, their terms of enlistment and even the movements of Kennebunk military companies throughout the war.

His diary tracked vital statistics such as marriages and deaths but also marriage customs and burial customs. Like a news reporter, he wrote of current events such as train wrecks or fires. He also gave biographical sketches of citizens. He recounted reports of the town selectmen and real estate transactions. He wrote of working conditions at the local shipyards and occasionally would insert poetry into his diary.

Rarely would he write from an emotional standpoint. His diary is more of a historical record than one of a personal nature. Andrew's last entry was written on August 13, 1897. His health had begun to deteriorate, and he soon died, at the age of ninety. Prior to his death, he transformed his mercantile into a place to house volumes of books and then donated it to the Free Library Association in memory of his daughter, Lucy. He also left $10,000 to the association for its maintenance.

His diaries somehow became the property of Civil War veteran Henry Fuller Curtis of Kennebunk. Although the date has not been recorded, these diaries were eventually sold by the Curtis family to Henry Parsons, who was responsible for the construction of the current Kennebunk Free Library. For a long time, these eleven volumes were placed in the care of Sylvia Cousens, until they were brought to the library in the 1960s by then president of the library board Mr. Nelson Hall. They have remained there ever since.

In 1986, through the efforts of a woman named Louise Walker Day, all of the volumes were photocopied to be used by the public. These were indexed in 1994 by a man named Leopold E. Hefner. They were bound in hardcover and now can be found in the reference section of the library. These volumes have also been microfilmed so that Andrew Walker's legacy can be enjoyed for years to come.

BOON ISLAND

Eight miles off the coast of York, Maine, is a small spit of land called Boon Island. Until recently, I had never heard of Boon Island.

There are very interesting stories associated with Boon Island. In 1682, a trading vessel, the *Increase*, was wrecked on the then unnamed island. The four survivors, three white men and one Indian, spent a month on the island, living on fish and gulls' eggs. Luckily, they had the ability to build a fire and were able to signal to the Indians on Mount Agamenticus who then came to

Boon Island. *Courtesy of the U.S. Coast Guard.*

rescue them. Believing that their survival was a boon granted from heaven, the men named the island Boon Island.

Boon Island itself is a rocky and desolate place. The island is about seven hundred by three hundred feet, fifteen feet or so above water, and has only a lighthouse, a solar panel, a generator/power building and the few remains of the lightkeepers quarters.

The most famous incident in the island's history was the wreck of the British ship *Nottingham Galley* on December 11, 1710. The *Nottingham Galley* was owned by a man named John Deane. The ship set sail from Ireland in 1710 with its cargo of cordage, butter and cheese, headed for Boston. After the ship wrecked on Boon Island, Deane and his surviving crew were marooned for twenty-six days, with only a piece of canvas to protect them from the elements. Although they could see the mainland from the island, they were unable to build a fire to make a distress signal. They survived initially on rockweed, mussels and a sea gull they managed to kill. Attempts to build a raft from the timber that washed ashore from the wreck failed. The ship's cook died, followed by the carpenter. The starving crew resorted to cannibalism to survive. As they had no means of building a fire, they ate the carpenter's body raw. The harrowing story was fictionalized by Kenneth Roberts in his novel *Boon Island*. The men were finally rescued after one of the rafts they had tried to build washed up on the shore in York. Men were sent out to investigate and discovered the survivors of the *Nottingham Galley*. In recent years, nine cannons from the *Nottingham Galley* have been salvaged from the ocean surrounding the island.

It was not until 1799 that the first tower was erected on Boon Island. It stood 50 feet tall, was made from wood and was unlighted. It survived until 1804, when it was destroyed in a violent storm. The following year, a stone "day beacon" was erected. Not until the winter of 1812 was a lighthouse built on the island, at a cost of $3,000. The lighthouse was authorized by President James Madison. This lighthouse was destroyed by a storm in 1831 and rebuilt the following year at a cost of $4,000. The present Boon Island Light was constructed between 1852 and 1854, along with a new dwelling. The masonry tower is 133 feet high, the tallest in New England. It is 25 feet in diameter at its base and 12 feet in diameter at the top.

Legends about the lives of the various keepers include one about a keeper from the nineteenth century who arrived at the island with his new bride. Within only a few months, the keeper became ill and died during a frightful storm. Knowing the importance of warning ships of the dangers of Boon Island, his wife climbed the tower's 168 stairs and lit the lamp for the duration of the storm, which lasted several days. Because the island is visible from the mainland, residents of York noticed the lack of light from the island following that storm and sailed out to investigate. It is reported that they discovered the young woman wandering the rocks aimlessly, driven mad by grief and exhaustion. She reportedly died a few weeks later.

In one Internet account of the island, I read that a ghost has been seen by many people on Boon Island. The ghost is described as a sad-looking young woman dressed all in white. Some people who claim to have seen the ghost believe that she is the mistress of Captain Deane of the ill-fated *Nottingham Galley*, while others claim that she is that young bride whose husband, the keeper, died shortly after they arrived on the island.

It must have been frightening for those who lived on the island during its manned lighthouse years. Some storms were reported to have had seventy-foot waves that crashed into the lighthouse tower.

The lighthouse was finally automated following the blizzard of 1978.

THE WITCH'S GRAVE

This spring, I received two separate e-mails regarding the so-called Witch's Grave in Kennebunk. I think it is an odd coincidence that these e-mails came right around the first day of spring, typically a celebrated time for witches or witch-wannabes. The Vernal Equinox, the first day of spring, is the time when the length of the day is equal to the length of the night. It is the official end of winter and the beginning of spring.

Years ago, I heard of the so-called Witch's Grave and its location on Sea Road. There is a small family plot, once surrounded by an iron fence and granite corner markers where a strange headstone once stood. The marker, with no names on it, was square in shape, stood about a foot tall and supposedly had devils' heads carved on it.

I had heard of strange ceremonies being performed there on dark evenings and wondered what those stories were all about. Now, after many years, the stone has vanished. The legends, as legends in New England have a tendency to do, have grown bigger and bigger. As we know, legends are many times just that—legends, not facts.

I have learned more about the grave and would like to try to dispel this one legend or rumor.

Roger Gonneville, the man to whom I dedicated my first book, was a well-loved citizen and avid historian. He meticulously researched many topics regarding Kennebunk history, from the trotting park to the Civil War memorial, and he even researched the Witch's Grave. He wrote detailed notes that now belong to his daughter, Gail.

When asked about the notes on the Witch's Grave, Roger refused to share them. His reason was not to protect the dead; it was to protect the living. Rather than cause any harm or sadness to living relatives of the individual buried beneath the unusual marker, Roger remained quiet.

I have learned, without mentioning age, sex or name, that the individual buried in the family cemetery was in fact afflicted with a mental illness or form of mental retardation. Because mental illness and retardation were so widely misunderstood in the nineteenth century, they carried with them a substantial social stigma or mark of shame. In many societies, including ours, the mentally ill were often blamed for bringing on their own illnesses, and many saw them as victims of bad fate, moral or religious transgression or witchcraft. In fact, disorders in early Egyptian, Indian, Greek and Roman writings show that the physicians and philosophers who contemplated problems of human

This carved stone monument that once marked the grave has long since disappeared.
Courtesy of the Brick Store Museum.

behavior regarded mental illness as a reflection of displeasure of the gods or as evidence of demonic possession.

In the case of the grave on Sea Road in Kennebunk, whether or not the family believed that their loved one was the victim of witchcraft will never be known. It is more likely that those with no understanding of mental illness believed it and created the myth. It is also more likely that the family of the individual buried in the so-called Witch's Grave wanted to protect their loved one after death by not marking the grave with a name or date. Their choice of gravestones was perhaps not that unusual.

Many believe that the faces on the stone were devils, but according to one website I visited, those who practice witchcraft revere nature and entirely reject any connection with the devil.

Another more likely description of the heads carved on the stone was offered to me recently. Perhaps they were meant to represent gargoyles. This notion fits the era, as gargoyles were popular symbols in gardens and architectural elements of the Renaissance Revival period in America. This is the era in which the individual buried there had lived and died. Gargoyles were symbols of protection. The family perhaps placed the stone on the grave with these figures to protect their loved one. I'd like to believe that is the case.

Perhaps now the legend, like the person buried in that cemetery, can finally be laid to rest.

At some point after 1994, the stone disappeared. It is believed to have been stolen. Perhaps some immoral person thought that it would make a nice garden decoration. Or perhaps someone grew tired of people believing that the individual in the grave was a witch and wanted the so-called ceremonies to stop. We may never know the answer.

THE KKK IN MAINE

When I think of the Ku Klux Klan, I think of the South, not Maine. I have recently learned that Maine, with 150,000 members in 1920, possessed the largest, most active Ku Klux Klan membership outside of the South. Rather than targeting African Americans, Maine Ku Klux Klan members targeted Franco-Americans.

What stirred my interest in this topic was a large roster of Klan members from Kennebunk that was found in the attic of Dan Boothby's

A local roster of KKK members in Maine.

house on High Street. Until Dan showed me the document, dated 1925, with fifteen local residents' names on it, I had no idea of the KKK history in Maine.

I began researching on the Internet and found that the Klan's presence here in Maine began with businessmen, bankers, ministers, politicians and newspaper editors. In 1920, an anti-language bill was easily passed in Maine that prohibited the teaching of subject matter in any other language than English in our public schools. This law was not overturned until 1976. Public

A vintage postcard shows KKK marchers in Milo, Maine.

school authorities of the era also found inventive ways to discourage French from being spoken on school grounds or in school corridors. By 1924, the KKK had elected a governor in Maine.

In Milo, Maine, the first Ku Klux Klan march to be held in New England took place in broad daylight in September 1923. In 1924, twenty thousand Portlanders marched in a parade in support of the KKK. In Brownville, Maine, that same year, a Ku Klux Klan member in full regalia led a motorcade of members to the Brownville Centennial Pageant Grounds as part of a ceremony to celebrate the town's 100th anniversary.

In one report, I read that Stephen King's wife's family changed their name from a French name to an Anglicized version because of the Ku Klux Klan in Maine.

With the large number of members in Maine, it is surprising to learn that the only reported violence of the era relating to the Klan came in the form of attacks against the Klan or Klan members themselves.

Klan organizing represented a dark period in our history. There are still small pockets of hate groups in Maine, but we must all ensure that they never again gain the momentum or membership numbers that the KKK had in the 1920s.

THE MURDER OF DR. SWETT

The movie industry typically portrays the Victorian era as a time of prim and proper behavior. Scenes from movies such as *Meet Me in St. Louis* come to mind. In reality, all generations and eras have their own scandals and problems.

In Kennebunk in 1866, there was quite a scandal.

As church bells rang on Sunday morning, September 23, 1866, the entire town was abuzz with the shocking news unfolding around them. Murder in Kennebunk! The victim was the well-known Dr. Charles Swett. The more shocking news was that the person sent to jail, charged with his murder, was none other than Jane Swett, his wife.

This seemingly upstanding couple lived at the corner of Sea Road and Summer Street and had two daughters. One was married and living in Kennebunkport, and the other was just fourteen and still living at home when the murder occurred. Dr. Swett was forty-eight years old at the time and Jane was fifty-one. She was accused of poisoning her husband to death with an excessive dose of morphine.

Dr. Swett. *Courtesy of the Brick Store Museum.*

The Dr. Swett home stands on the corner of Sea Road and Summer Street in Kennebunk. *Courtesy of the Brick Store Museum.*

When the trial began, the public soon learned what troubled circumstances lay just beneath the surface of this strange case. The doctor, who had been practicing medicine for some time, had no formal training. What he knew as a doctor he had learned as a veterinary assistant to his father.

Dr. Swett was a member of the local temperance society, which promoted sobriety. Unfortunately, as many witnesses testified, the doctor was often drunk in public. He also had frequent drunken quarrels with his wife.

Increase Kimball, the attorney for the state, tried to prove that Jane had deliberately poisoned her husband. As the trial progressed, however, doubt was cast that it was an intentional act at all.

Reports claimed that in addition to his drinking, Dr. Swett often self-medicated with morphine and was in fact an addict. He often told of his use of morphine to rid himself of the effects of alcohol. Was Jane simply trying to expedite a cure for a hangover?

Another item reported was that the doctor was often found in the company of strange women and was rumored to be having an affair with a woman named Mrs. Mary Anne Hutchings. Jane apparently had knowledge of the affair.

The youngest daughter was put on the stand and testified that her mother and father constantly quarreled. She said that at one point she had witnessed her father put his hands around her mother's throat. However, on the day her father died, she testified that it was her mother who had sent her to fetch the hidden whiskey bottle from the barn where her father kept it. She told the jury that she saw her mother take a white piece of paper from her apron and pour its contents into the whiskey bottle, which she then shook vigorously. Her mother then told her to return the bottle to where she had found it. When her father went out to the barn, he drank the tainted whiskey and returned to the front parlor, where he collapsed on the sofa. Her mother summoned a neighbor for help, but that neighbor had come and believed that Dr. Swett was merely drunk, so he left.

Dr. Lemuel Richards was called next and, upon his arrival, found Dr. Swett in a coma. As he attended to Dr. Swett, Mrs. Swett told him that she had poisoned him but that it had been an accident. She also claimed to have taken forty grams of morphine herself and would soon be dead, too. Her husband expired at the scene, but she lived.

During the trial, it was also learned that five months earlier the doctor had sold his interest in the home and property to his wife for $500. Several witnesses testified that Jane was trying to sell the property at the time of his death to be free of him when the murder occurred.

In the end, the jury took ten and a half hours to reach a verdict. They found Jane Swett guilty of murder and sentenced her to six years at the prison in Thomaston.

Although in prison, she did manage to sell the home to a man named Timothy Hubbard. It was just one year later, on Valentine's Day 1867. Town Historian Andrew Walker recorded in his diary that Jane Swett lived in the poorhouse in Kennebunk when she was released from prison. He also recorded that she died there but that her body was buried next to that of her husband at the Landing Cemetery.

TRAGIC DEATH OF LIZZIE BOURNE

Mount Washington has been a popular tourist destination for over 150 years. Long before the road was built to the top of the mountain and the cog railroad built to reach the summit, there were only walking trails for hikers to climb. The extreme environment on this mountain sometimes produces winds in excess of 231 miles per hour and has claimed many lives over the decades. The story surrounding the death of one victim is known to many but bears repeating. It is the story of a young Kennebunk woman named Lizzie Bourne.

Lizzie was the daughter of a prominent judge named Edward Emerson Bourne. She was twenty-three years old in 1855, when she was invited to

George Bourne, builder of
the Wedding Cake House in
Kennebunk. *Courtesy of the Brick
Store Museum.*

A photograph of Lizzie Bourne.
Courtesy of the Brick Store Museum.

climb the mountain by her uncle George. George W. Bourne was known locally as the builder of the Wedding Cake House. Her uncle intended to take Lizzie and his own daughter to the top of the mountain and stay at the Tip Top House, which had been built there only two years earlier.

The threesome began their ascent late in the morning due to a slight morning rain that slowly cleared. Dressed in the attire of the era, Lizzie was weighed down by the yards of fabric that made up her skirts, petticoats, pantaloons and stockings.

A fierce September wind also slowed their progress. As darkness fell, the weather became increasingly worse. When the group stopped to rest, Lizzie's uncle tried to buffer the wind by creating a small wall of rocks. He was not able to tell how much farther they needed to climb to reach the summit because the mountain had become enveloped in clouds and darkness.

When they decided to carry on, George and his daughter were horrified to discover that in the bitter cold, frail and exhausted Lizzie had passed away. There was nothing they could do for her. She had died from exposure, possibly heart failure. They stayed by her body until the morning light.

When they awoke in the morning, they could clearly see the Tip Top House standing a very short distance away. What a tragic sense of failure must have enveloped them when they saw how close they had been when Lizzie died.

Her body was transported down the mountain and returned to Kennebunk, where she was buried. Judge Bourne had a large stone monument carved for her that he hoped to have placed on the mountain where she died. Unfortunately, there was no way to carry it up the mountain, so he had it placed on her grave in Hope Cemetery instead.

Currently, a wooden marker stands on the spot where she died. Over one hundred persons have died on the mountain since her passing. She was neither the first nor the last, but a lesson is to be learned about how quickly the weather can turn deadly on Mount Washington.

The Tip Top House was destroyed by fire in 1908, and in 1938 the Mount Washington Observatory was built in its place.

THE DOC SNOW GANG

This story began at a Portland Ephemera show. Every so often, I will attend one of these events to look for old photographs, letters or postcards relating

A vintage postcard photograph of the Doc Snow house in Dayton, Maine.

to York County. Several dealers put up display booths and fill a hall with thousands of paper collectibles.

At one particular show, I purchased a postcard that had a photograph of an old farm and a caption that read, "Home of the Doc Snow Gang, Dayton, Maine." In the sleeve of the plastic covering was tucked a yellowed newspaper clipping. The article was dated 1911 and had the following heading: "No Trace of Body Can Be Found." I decided to try to learn more about this home's past. What I uncovered was a bizarre story about a family that once lived in Dayton.

Back in the winter and spring of 1911, more than forty summer homes were broken into and items were stolen. These homes were located in Salmon Falls, Kennebunkport, Waterboro, Bar Mills and more. Finally, after receiving a tip, the sheriff gathered a posse and went to the home of Doc Snow in Dayton.

Doc Snow was a veterinarian by trade. He and his wife lived in their home with their three children on Hight Road in Dayton, not far from the present-day Route 5. When deputies arrived, Doc Snow resisted arrest and fired a gun at one of the deputies. As he was being led from the house, his wife, Maud, was arriving by buggy. Doc Snow shouted to her to take a gun and shoot the deputies, but she too was arrested. Both were jailed in Alfred at the York County Jail. Their children were taken in by neighbors.

As the news unfolded, two other gang members were arrested. The Snow home was searched, and wagonloads of stolen articles were discovered. Many of the homeowners came to claim their property.

Snow turned state's evidence and confessed. He gave testimony against the other two gang members and told prosecutors that they would steal the property and then sell it in secondhand shops. He remained in jail until his sentencing.

His wife was released and returned to her children. Within three months, she was again sent to the county jail in Alfred. This time, she was charged with being an accomplice to murder. Apparently, Mrs. Snow's three children, the oldest about nine years old, told law officials that they had witnessed the murder of a man named Charles Weymouth two years earlier in their kitchen. They gave gruesome details of Weymouth being beaten by two men named Joseph Buzzell and Olney Merrill. They claimed that their mother had cleaned up the blood from the kitchen floor. They further stated that Weymouth's body had been stuffed into a wooden box and disposed of in the nearby woods.

Maud Snow claimed that her children were simply making up stories. Doc Snow, still in the county jail, also denied that the murder had taken place and said that Weymouth had simply left town because he owed too many people money.

For days, officers combed the woods and swamps around the Snows' property and dug holes in their yard. They even dragged a portion of the Saco River but were unable to find a body. An angry mob of Dayton citizens threatened to tear down the Snow home when finally a break came in the case.

A mail carrier named Hewes claimed that Weymouth was alive and living in Canada. Sure enough, after an exhaustive search, he was indeed found alive and well in Sherbrooke, Canada. The story had been a complete fabrication by the children.

Maud and her husband and one of the other so-called gang members were released from prison. What became of the fourth man is unclear. He was probably left "holding the bag," so to speak, and remained in jail.

Maud and her husband and children returned home and lived out their days. The home still stands to this day.

THE CAT MILL

According to oral tradition, the Mousam River takes its name from an Indian word or phrase. The actual meaning of the word varies, depending on which history you read on the subject. Historian George GilPatrick claimed that it meant "moose."

The Cat Mill. *Courtesy of the Brick Store Museum.*

In Kennebunk, there is a road called the Cat Mousam Road. There are at least two stories that tell the supposed origin of this name. The old-timers of Wells and Kennebunk no doubt have heard both legends. Both legends support the theory that the name came from a mill that used to stand on the river years ago. It was called the Cat Mill.

Just below the Mill Street Bridge in West Kennebunk, you can see a small building that currently belongs to the Kennebunk Light and Power District. This little shed sits atop the footings of the original Cat Mill.

The Cat Mill was a sawmill. The mill shown in the accompanying photo is the last mill of many that were built on the very same site. One was destroyed by flood, and one was destroyed by Indians. The one in the photo was destroyed by fire in 1904.

As early as 1752, a deed mentions "the saw mill called the Cat Mill." Daniel Remich, an early historian, relates two versions of the legend of the mill in his book *History of Kennebunk*. You can decide which one to believe.

The first states that the workmen employed at the mill on these falls were annoyed by a group of youngsters that continually threw rocks and played pranks on the workmen and often stole their lunches. One of the workmen finally gave the boys a very harsh scolding and ordered them off the premises. This man had a beloved cat. Unfortunately, upon returning to work the following day, he discovered that the youths had killed his cat by hanging it from the mill's rafters. He reportedly "wept like a child" at his loss. It is told that this event gave the mill its name.

The second story, less credible, also involves a cat. This story tells of the workmen of the mill being very superstitious individuals who were often visited at the mill yard by a cat. This cat had a peculiar habit of sitting on the logs as they were being sawn, only to jump free of the blade just in time to avoid injury. On one occasion, it slipped and had one paw taken off by the saw. The cat immediately disappeared into the woods. The next morning, it was ascertained that a woman in the vicinity had lost a hand during the preceding night. It was therefore concluded that she must be a witch who had taken the form of the cat and been mutilated at the sawmill.

Whatever the true source of the unusual name, it certainly can cause confusion to newcomers and directory assistance operators nowadays.

THE KING'S MARKER

This spring I went in search of a rock—not just any old rock, but an important rock that served as a mile marker on what was once known as the King's Highway.

In the early days of colonial Massachusetts, of which Maine was a part, the governing body of the Massachusetts Bay Colony complained of the lack of decent roads when they needed to travel to the state to hold court. So, in 1653, the inhabitants of Wells, York and Kittery were ordered to "make straight and convenient pathways along the east coast for man and horse." Towns were fined for not maintaining these roads.

These early roads were, however, merely pathways with ruts for carts (of which there were very few) and a path in the middle of the ruts for horses. In those days, travel was difficult. It is recorded that in 1725, the distance from Boston to Falmouth took an average of twelve days to cover by horseback.

In 1760, when the colonial post was set up, the highway began to improve. Over time, 129 markers were placed at one-mile intervals between Portland and Boston. An extension of the road also ran from Portland to Machias. The miles were measured by a new invention of Benjamin Franklin's called the odometer. The markers were all inscribed with a *B*, or the word "Boston" in some cases, and the number of miles from that point to Boston. Some were

A vintage photo of the King's Highway marker prior to the development of the neighborhood.

A present-day photograph of the King's Highway marker.

A close-up of the marker.

carved in granite posts, some in slate and most in large stones. These markers helped postal riders and stagecoach drivers maintain their schedules.

Approximately one dozen of the markers from Boston to Machias have been located. More have been lost forever to time, and some still are waiting to be found.

The one I was looking for is in Wells. It has been a well-known historical marker in that town for years. But I had never seen it, and the information I had to go on was a dated photo and even more dated directions. The directions made little sense because the area has been heavily developed since my photo was taken. I looked near brooks and bushes and finally found it in, of all places, somebody's front yard.

This particular mile marker is inscribed with a *B* for Boston and the mileage "89," as well as the year 1769. If you are looking for tangible evidence of our colonial past, the pathways of early New England, take a drive up the Captain Thomas Road and bear right onto Old County Road (or Old King's Highway). Not far up, on your right, in front of the home shown in the accompanying photo, you will find this ancient marker.

THE REAL SCARLET LETTER

New England has a wealth of fascinating history. Some of it has become the subject of books by famous authors. One story that comes to mind is by Nathaniel Hawthorne, entitled *The Scarlet Letter*. In this story, written in 1850, a woman named Hester Prynne was punished by a court for committing adultery. She was ordered to wear an embroidered scarlet letter *A* on the bodice of her clothing at all times when in public. Interestingly enough, there is a considerable amount of evidence that Hawthorne created Hester Prynne based on a woman named Mary Bachiler, who lived in Kittery, Maine, in 1648.

Captain William Hawthorne, immigrant ancestor of the distinguished novelist, was rewarded with 870 acres of prime land on the Piscataqua River three farms north of Mary Bachiler. Years later, Nathaniel Hawthorne, noted as an avid scholar of colonial history, soaked up local history during extended visits to the Kittery area. His journal does not mention the name of Bachiler but does note a young woman doomed to wear the letter *A* on the breast of her gown under an old colony law as punishment for adultery. A book published in 1910 to commemorate the Eliot centennial states that Mary Beedle Bachiler was the woman from whom Hawthorne patterned the heroine of *The Scarlet Letter*.

Mary Beedle, a widow, kept house for Reverend Stephen in the year 1648. He was sixty years her senior. Bachiler, the founder of Hampton, New Hampshire, had moved to land just below that of Mary Beedle along the banks of the Piscataqua River. He came there in 1647, following his excommunication from his parish in Hampton for repeated dissention. Because his neighbors thought it unseemly that Mary keep house for him, he married her. The exact date of Stephen's marriage to Mary is unknown because he performed the ceremony and failed to publish it, an omission for which he was fined five pounds. Mary was his fourth wife.

In 1651, Mary was convicted of having an affair with a neighbor named George Roberts. According to Herbert Sylvester in "Romance of the Maine Coast," she was subsequently sentenced by the Georgiana (York) court to be flogged and branded with the letter *A*. George Rogers also was to be "flogged with forty stripes save one. Mary was to receive hers at the first Kittery Town Meeting six weeks after the birth of her child by George Rogers." The court also ordered Stephen Bachiler and Mary to live together as man and wife, even though they sought to divorce. Instead, Bachiler took refuge with his grandson in Hampton. By 1654, he had returned to England.

Three years later, Mary was again in court for living with a man not her husband, named Thomas Hanscom. She was barred from marrying him. She was finally granted a divorce from Bachiler in 1656. "She told the court that Stephen Bachiler had gone to England where he had taken another wife and she said she needed freedom to remarry for assistance in raising her two ailing children, and to conserve her estate." In 1657, she married Thomas Turner and became a respectable, successful, churchgoing woman, active in community affairs.

Truth is often stranger than fiction.

KEEPING UP WITH MADELYN MARX

Every now and then, I like to interview folks who have lived in our area for most of their lives to get a good sense of what makes up the fabric of our communities—the human side, our living histories, so to speak.

I met with a Kennebunk Beach resident named Madelyn Marx, who is well known in Kennebunk. Madelyn welcomed me into her home on Great Hill Road, which winds along the beach. She has lived here in this same home since 1958 but was born and raised on Sea Road in a home next to what she called "Izzy Maling's garage." That garage was long ago converted into a home but can be distinguished by its white-washed cinder block façade. Relatives still own the home in which she was raised.

Madelyn's mother came from Nova Scotia, and her father hailed from Montreal. Although both spoke French, they did not teach their children to speak it. Madelyn's father, Archibald Arthur Nedeau, was an ice delivery man in the days before refrigeration. He was known as Pete. He would chop the ice himself on a pond in Wells and store it in an icehouse filled with sawdust. The ice would last for its delivery during the summer season. His delivery route was along the seaside and to the houses of Kennebunk Beach. Madelyn's mother was named Elizabeth. She was a stay-at-home mom, according to Madelyn, who, among other things, was a wonderful cook and made a delicious meringue pie.

As a child, Madelyn attended local schools and remembers many of her teachers, including Mr. Thyng, Miss Landry and Miss Burleigh. Like many kids of her day, she remembers riding her bike to the beach, playing baseball in the summer and sledding in the winters. To this day, she still enjoys baseball.

Madelyn Marx at her home on
Great Hill Road in Kennebunk.

In her youth, what is now called Mother's Beach was referred to as the
Dipsy Beach because that is where the Dipsy bathhouse used to be. Also,
what is known now as Strawberry Island on the Great Hill Road was never
called that when she was growing up. It was always referred to as Libby's
Point. There was actually a house at the end of the strip of land where Mr.
Libby lived. It had a grand piano in it that Madelyn can still hear him play.
The old house became vacant following Mr. Libby's death and eventually
burned down in 1963. Arson was suspected.

Upon graduation from high school in 1942, she took a position as a
secretary for Judge Bourne. It was during this time that she met her future
husband Robert (Bob) Marx. They were married in 1945 in Judge Bourne's
office. Bob can be remembered by many as the chief of the state police.
He was twice appointed to the position by Senator Edmund Muskie, who
was then the governor of Maine. Muskie and Bob were also good friends
and golfing buddies. In 1947, as fires raged in Maine, Bob was in charge
when the fires jumped the turnpike and threatened the town of Kennebunk.
Madelyn and many other women manned the building now known as the
Dorothy Stevens Center, where they made sandwiches for the firefighters.

Madelyn Marx, with the old Libby home in the background.

The center stood behind the Kennebunk Free Library at that time. It has since been moved to West Kennebunk.

Over the years, Madelyn has been involved in a large number of civic projects. She was one of a handful of people to begin the Kennebunk Conservation Commission and is widely respected as a pioneer in land preservation efforts. In 1999, the Kennebunk Land Trust, in recognition of her many accomplishments, honored her by naming fourteen acres of pristine tidal river marshes and uplands the Madelyn Marx Preserve.

She has also been heavily involved in politics through the years. She served as the secretary for the Kennebunk Republican Committee for twenty-five years. In her living room, there are signed photos of George H.W. Bush and George W. Bush. She has been very involved in the Maine Cancer Society as well. Another group that she is part of is the Kennebunk Coastal Property Owners Association. This group's mission statement reads: "To preserve, protect and enhance the natural beauty and attractiveness of the area known as Kennebunk Beach." This group has been meeting for about twenty years now and has approximately four hundred members. Madelyn has been the association's secretary for the last ten years.

From the number of birthday cards I spotted in her living room during my visit, I imagine she is well known and well loved throughout the community.

She is certainly one of the most energetic and kind people I have met. She is an example to us all.

NELSON WENTWORTH

One of the residents of Kennebunk who grew up in that small town was gracious enough to share his experiences with me. Although history tends to focus on long-ago events, I always realize that we are creating history ourselves, each and every day. By telling his story, Nelson Wentworth made me realize how fast things become outdated. My own children do not know some of the things I remember from my youth. Thus history is created.

Nelson was born on January 26, 1932. As a kid, he didn't remember having any particular views about girls except that they should be neat, nice and friendly. The only slang he can recall was used among his musician friends, who thought it was cool to greet each other with "Hey Man." Nicknames

Nelson Wentworth (middle) with two friends, circa 1955.

weren't that important during his years in high school. No family member or teacher ever called him by a nickname. However, he does remember being called "Nellie" on the baseball field in high school and college. Not until later did his band leader begin calling him "Junior," and later still he gained a temporary nickname of Nelson "Stardust" Wentworth after a popular tune of the day that he and his band often played. In fact, his band was called the Stardusters.

During high school, his hobbies were music and sports. He played in the school band, ran cross-country, played baseball and basketball and ran track. He didn't play football. He claims that he was probably too short, but the real truth, he said, was that he didn't relish the idea of getting killed.

In his recollection, there were no real discipline problems in school. In fact, he remembers only once having a point taken off his daily score for not paying attention, and that, he claims, was discipline enough to last six years! The teachers he had were interested, supportive, caring, thoughtful and friendly.

His father was strict but fair. He always took an interest in everything that Nelson did in school and college. In spite of chronic ill health, his father attended just about every game, concert or play that Nelson was in. Although he died at the very young age of fifty-eight, Nelson told me that his dad was the most special man that he ever knew and that he still thinks of him every day.

His idols of youth were those in the music industry, like Tommy Dorsey. He went to the Old Orchard Pier Ballroom to see big bands play on Saturday nights. He wanted to play and sound just like Tommy Dorsey and commented, "That was before I realized that no one could ever play and sound like Tommy Dorsey!" He collected many records and spent hours listening and playing along on the trombone. On weekends, he would take the train up to Portland and walk uptown to the music store, listen to records, buy one or two and then take the train home. In the 1950s, he felt that the cutting edge of music was bebop and progressive jazz. His father didn't care for it and called it "noise, just noise."

At age thirteen, Nelson began playing with dance bands. He played trombone and sang, continuing in later years in ballrooms and nightclubs on the coast of Florida. He stopped playing in 1961, when he became the principal of a school in Lantana, Florida. To Nelson, music had taken a rapid decline after Elvis, who "sounded like a wounded, whining hound dog." Today's music Nelson likens to noise on the Maine Turnpike. Or, as his dad used to say, "noise, just noise."

Nelson Wentworth
playing trombone
at the Log Cabin
Ballroom in Arundel.

Nelson also traveled to Boston several times in his youth to see the Red Sox play. His heroes of the baseball field were Ted Williams, Johnny Pesky, Dom DiMaggio and Bobby Doerr. He and his father went all the way to Melrose, Massachusetts, to watch a World Series game from Boston on TV in 1948.

Drive-in theatres became popular in the 1950s, and many homes began to get television sets. He saw his first TV from the showroom window of Green's Garage on Garden Street in Kennebunk. Managers left it on after 6:00 p.m. each day so that people could see what television looked like. When TV was new, family and friends would come over to watch it together. There were only two or three channels; often they were snowy, and it was hard to make out what was on the screen. *The Ed Sullivan Show* was a big favorite, along with Jack Benny and Charlie McCarthy, whose show was on Sunday nights. *Playhouse 90* was a favorite dramatic program on Thursday nights, and it was live, so you could see all of the mistakes and miscues.

For kids, the popular clothing items were gray flannel pants and white buck shoes. If you were a musician like Nelson, you would wear a sports coat without a collar or lapels and a big floppy bow tie. It also helped your image to wear your hair a little long so that it could be combed back on both sides to look just like a "duck's behind." He wore a necktie to school every day, as all boys did. No boy would even consider wearing a hat in school. Girls wore long skirts and penny-loafer shoes. Cardigan sweaters were sometimes turned so that the buttons were in the back. No one wore jeans to school. He knew of only three boys who smoked cigarettes and two boys who were rumored to have tried beer.

When he graduated from high school in 1950, the Korean War had begun. Because he had already been accepted to attend the Gorham State Teachers College, he was deferred from the military draft. Others weren't so lucky. His friend Robert Jackson was killed soon after arriving in Korea in 1951.

Nelson watched the McCarthy hearings on television at college. President Truman became one of his favorite Americans. The Eisenhower years were referred to in later generations as boring, but to Nelson and his wife, Margie, they were anything but boring! Nelson was married in 1952, and his first son was born in 1953. During that time, he played four years of college baseball, directed the college band, formed his own dance band and completed his student teaching.

Nelson graduated in 1954 and took his first job as principle in Owls Head, Maine. He then moved to Florida and taught fifth and sixth grades in West Palm Beach from 1956 to 1961. He and his wife built their first home in 1958 and had their second son in 1960. He then took the job in Lantana, Florida, as a principal.

When Nelson retired, he and Margie decided to move back to Kennebunk. "It just seemed like it was time". They live on the Sea Road now, and Nelson has been involved with the high school alumni. Both he and Margie enjoy seeing old friends again.

Thanks, Nelson. It is always fun to hear about the past! I'm sure his recollections will hit a familiar chord with many folks in Kennebunk and all of the small towns nearby.

ROBERT CANNEY SR.

There is a man named Robert Canney Sr. who has lived in Berwick with his wife, Claire, for over forty years now. Canney, a veteran, enlisted in

Robert Canney Sr.

the service in 1943 during the height of World War II when he was just seventeen years old. He managed to come through the war unharmed and decided to enlist for a second term. This, he recounts, may have been a very big mistake, because although the war hadn't killed him, the years following the war nearly did.

Canney was sent to the Pacific, where he was a radio man with the 403rd Troop Carrier Group and 63rd Troop Carrier Squadron. There, while on a flight from Guam in 1946, the plane's engines failed. The five-man crew was forced to crash-land in the ocean. Luckily, all survived the crash, and they were able to inflate two life rafts.

Canney remembers the ocean being as smooth as glass and that it took ten minutes for the plane to sink. Robert was alone in his life raft. The crew attempted to tie the two rafts together, but sometime during the night they came apart. When he awoke, the other raft and crewmembers were nowhere to be seen.

Panic must have set in. He remembers screaming aloud to no one and thinking that he might not survive. The ocean, no longer calm, began producing ten- and twelve-foot waves that pummeled his raft for two days. Finally, he was spotted by a rescue plane. His crew was also rescued over six miles away. That experience was harrowing to be sure, but what he would have to endure in the future would be far worse.

It was later that same year that Canney, while running to his plane, collapsed on the runway. He was diagnosed with pneumonia and taken to Fort McKinley Hospital in Manila. There he was told that he had tuberculosis and a lung fungus. For treatment, he would have to return to the United States. Coincidentally, while flying home for treatment, the plane he was on flew through the fallout of a hydrogen bomb test that had just been conducted on Bikini Atoll the previous day.

Upon arrival at Hickam Field in Hawaii, he had his first attack of malaria and lapsed into a coma. The coma lasted for four days. He recovered briefly, only to have a second attack of malaria, which again put him into a coma. This one also lasted for four days. After three weeks, Robert was able to continue his journey back to the United States. He finally arrived at Moore General Hospital in North Carolina.

While there, he volunteered to take an experimental drug called 7618, which had been recently developed by the British. This cured him of malaria, but the tuberculosis was still active. By 1947, he was transferred to a tropical disease hospital in Oteen, North Carolina. In this hospital, there were over eighteen hundred men with tuberculosis, malaria and other tropical diseases.

He underwent an experimental surgery in which twenty-four Lucite balls were inserted in the upper half of his left lung. It was hoped that these balls would displace the lung's capacity for oxygen, thus hampering the spread of his tuberculosis. Sixteen patients underwent this same surgery and all but Robert died from infection. The November issue of *Life* magazine in 1948 detailed this procedure and provided images of Robert's X-rayed lung. Unfortunately, by 1948 it was determined that the tuberculosis had spread to his right lung as well.

This time, he was operated on twice, and six ribs on his right side were removed to collapse his lung. The theory was that collapsing his lung would hamper the spread of the disease. Finally, he was given yet another experimental drug called streptomycin. He endured a total of nine hundred injections before beginning to show signs of improvement.

Next, he began a regime of physical therapy to regain his strength. After four years and six months in the hospital, he was finally released in 1950. He was told that they were sending him home with a five-year chance of survival.

In five years' time he had married Claire Nute and settled in Berwick, Maine. Since then, he has surpassed everyone's expectations and led a full life. He has written sixteen books on genealogy and taken out sixteen patents while working as an engineer for General Electric.

In 1990, Robert had a pacemaker put in and now jokes that he "has a plastic lung and a tin heart." He never had the Lucite balls removed for, after all, "they weren't bothering anyone."

Nowadays, you can run into Robert at one of the several air shows hosted by the Collings Foundation. This foundation has restored several vintage planes, including a B-17 Flying Fortress, B-24 Liberator and B-25 Mitchell Bomber. The foundation flies them to various locations nationwide for exhibit. Robert was gracious enough to get me a ride on a B-25 while the foundation was in Portland, Maine. That's another story!

You can also find Robert and Claire at the Maine Diner having lunch most weekdays. A remarkable life and a remarkable man!

THE LOSS OF THE *THRESHER*

Where were you in 1963? I was a small child, so I have vague recollections of that era. I know that the Cold War was raging and that it was a decade of changes that included one presidential assassination, race riots, peace demonstrations and an Apollo space mission.

I do remember the Cuban Missile Crisis of 1962 because I was in South Florida at the time and saw what seemed like thousands of U.S. planes flying overhead. There were so many that it almost looked like a swarm of bees in the skies above me. I remember that some had square-shaped tail sections, and only later in life did I learn that those were "Flying Boxcars," known as Fairchild C-119s.

While at a local antiques show, I came across a box of old newspaper clippings that told of a man named Alan Sinnott, who was the brother of Mrs. Benjamin Nest. The date was April 1963. As I read the story, I realized that an event of national importance had happened that month. That event took on a more local and personal nature here in York County.

That sad event was the loss of the nuclear submarine USS *Thresher* with all hands onboard. Alan Sinnott was one of them. A second clipping told of another local man who was transferred off the *Thresher* just prior to its loss. These clippings held the story, too, of Harry Joyce, who had served on the *Thresher* since 1958. The Sunday before its sinking, Harry had taken his ten-year-old son on a tour of the ship. There were 129 men onboard when the sub went down, most of them local men.

Arundel woman's brother on Thresher *...nued on Page 12)*

...a time ...end we dislike, it is the...

...arry Joyce transferred to 'Jack' from 'Thresher' in Jan.

PO/1C ALAN D. SINNETT

Mrs. Benjamin Nest of Ardel is one of those bereaved the loss of the ....clear subn rine Thres... week. H... brother, ...ty Offic... Alan ..., Con... ...on ...week

went down. About fifteen men he knew by name only. The rest were his friends, the men he had worked with and lived with for more than a year and a half.

He would have been aboard the Thresher himself except that fate and the Navy intervened and transferred him to the USS Jack, presumably a faster, quieter and deeper diving submarine soon to be launched at Kittery.

To Harry Joyce, who has served aboard submarines since 1943, the Thresher was the "finest ship I've ever been on." Her crew was "a wonderful bunch; one of the best groups of men I've ever known. They were outstanding."

He is well qualified to hold such opinions. He had known fine crews before. In fact he was at the helm of the submarine Sea Lion when she sank the Japanese battleship Kongo Maru, crippled another Japanese battleship and sank two Japanese destroyers, part of a major Japanese task force encountered by the Sea Lion and her crew on the China Sea in 1944 and sunk by them with one salvo and ten to peadces fired from the surface. Many times he has been nearly out submarines which were during the years he has spent aboard su"But we were lucky — he w always able to regain contro!

CPO HARRY JOYCE

The week past has been a sad one along the southern coast of Maine. In every little town there are those who lost friends when the Thresher went down last Wednesday. In many of the towns husbands, fathers and b others were lost. But there is at least ne family whose sadness can mixed with thankful ness ...t is the family of Henry Joyce ...irch Hill Road, York. ...ry Joyce was Chief Elec Technician aboard the ...er from the time she was ...sioned until January 23, ...n he was transferred to the soon- ...ities aboard the ....hed USS Jack ...the enlisted men ....she

(Continued on Page 7)

18, 1963 ...d ...ered USS Jack? ... "I have some reservations ...serving aboard the nuclear-pow ...t which are natural at a time like ...this," he said. "But I'm going ...out on the Jack and that's about ...e ...it. The Jack should be at least ...as good a ship as the Thresher, ... if she is I'll be satisfied." ...aid, ...ber incident have not ...ibt the integrity of ...I'm going out ...expect to take ...r's test ...uld

Faded newspaper clippings tell of the loss of crewmen aboard the *Thresher*.

As a tribute to those men and all onboard, I will write their story again.

On April 10, 1963, the USS *Thresher* left Kittery for deep-diving exercises. In addition to its sixteen officers and ninety-six enlisted men, the submarine carried seventeen civilian technicians to observe its performance. The *Thresher* was built in 1958 at the Portsmouth Naval Yard in nearby Kittery, Maine. On this voyage, it was accompanied by the USS *Skylark*. At nine o'clock that morning, they were about two hundred miles off the coast of Cape Cod when the *Thresher* began its trials.

At 9:13 a.m., the *Skylark* received a signal that the *Thresher* was experiencing minor difficulties. Listeners on the *Skylark* next heard something on their underwater listening devices that sounded like air rushing into an air tank and then silence.

Efforts to make contact with the *Thresher* failed, and a search group was formed in an attempt to find the sub. The USS *Recovery* located what remained of the ship, fourteen hundred fathoms deep. That is approximately eighty-five hundred feet.

Photos taken indicate that it is in six pieces on the sea floor. There were no survivors. The official report given was that the *Thrasher* suffered a catastrophic mechanical failure. The cause of the failure is unknown.

Because of its nuclear reactor, the site is regularly monitored for any release of radioactivity from the nuclear fuel components. Monitoring operations in 1965, 1977, 1983 and 1986 indicated that the *Thresher* has not had a significant effect on the radioactivity of its surroundings.

The event touched so many lives in Southern Maine. Mothers, fathers and other relatives still remember the faces of their loved ones who perished. Many children grew up not knowing their dads because of this tragic event, and some are now parents themselves.

TWO MYSTERIES IN ELIOT

A friend of mine told me a story about a home that she once owned in Eliot, Maine. It is a curious story with two mysteries still unsolved. The home is located on the State Road near South Eliot and was purchased by Pat Joseph and her former husband in 1977.

Immediately upon moving in, a peculiar situation presented itself. While looking around the property, Pat went into the barn and noticed that the previous owners had left behind two very large jars. Being a lover of old things, she thought she might clean them up and use them somehow in her new home. She removed the lid from one to see what it contained and found it full of an unusual, powdery substance. Upon sifting through the substance, she soon realized, to her horror, that these two jars contained cremated human remains!

Not knowing what to do with two jars of someone's beloved (or maybe not so beloved) family members, she called the local mortuary, which agreed to take them off her property and dispose of them properly. Unfortunately, she wasn't able to find out whose remains they were or who had left them in the barn.

In the following years, like many people who buy old homes, Pat delved into the history of the property and researched old deeds. This information gave her dates and names of previous owners, and she learned that the home was originally built about 1810 by one of Eliot's early residents whose last name was Remich.

Also, like many folks who buy old properties, Pat decided to remodel some of the rooms. First, she removed the wallpaper in the living room. Long an annoyance, this wall, with its horsehair plaster, bulged in a particular area. Pat removed the plaster and repaired the spot. To her dismay, hiding behind the plaster was a pair of very old brass knuckles!

Her first thought was who in the world would plaster brass knuckles into a wall? Her second, and more unsettling, question was why?

In time, they sold this home and moved to Kennebunk. They brought the brass knuckles with them. When Pat showed them to me, my curiosity ran amok. We both decided to do some digging and see what we might turn up in old newspapers or vital records of Eliot.

Unfortunately, our sleuthing has led us nowhere, and we have come up empty-handed, except for one newspaper account from the late 1700s. Eerily, an old court document relates to a case in Eliot in which a man beat his wife so severely that it caused her death. For this offence, he was fined five pounds.

Although we aren't sure that this incident ties into the old home in any way, it certainly gives us pause, and we are very happy that we did not live in that era!

The Remich homestead in Eliot, Maine.

THE ALFRED JAIL

While reading through old newspapers, I was surprised to read how many times someone had committed suicide while in prison at the old jail in Alfred, Maine.

I have driven by the old jail on Route 111 in Alfred several times. It is a desolate-looking brick building. The jail was built as the York County Jail in 1869–70 but has not operated as a jail in many years and, until recently, stood vacant and dark.

I was able to tour the old jail and take photos. The jail was originally constructed with two halves. The front half was for the guard's kitchen and living spaces and the back half was for housing prisoners. The prisoners' section consisted of a three-story cellblock.

In the guard's quarters on the first floor, there was a small hole in the wall used to pass food through to the prisoners from the kitchen. The second floor was the entrance to the jail via a large set of wooden steps. A main reception area just inside the entrance was used to process the prisoners' admittance to the jail. This area was the first thing a prisoner would see upon entering to serve his or her time. Surprisingly, remnants of lovely Victorian wallpaper still cling to the wall here. High ceilings and decorative trim also remain, in stark contrast to the cellblock within the second half of the building.

The third floor was the residence of the prison's warden. Again, remnants of floral wallpaper could still be seen here. This floor also had its own kitchen and an office. The office had a steel-plated hole on the wall—an eerie reminder that from here, the warden could look through to the cellblocks to keep an eye on the prisoners.

The actual entrance to the cellblock was on the second floor via a large steel door. This steel door led to yet another door, circular in shape and made of bars. The second floor also had steel peepholes in the wall through which the guards could look over the cellblock.

As I entered the cellblock area, I could immediately sense the feeling of doom that this place must have invoked in its day. Each cell, with two-foot-wide doors, was a small chamber with suspended metal beds and a communal latrine in the center. The cells were dark and freezing cold, with paint flaking off every surface. The first-floor cells were so dark that you could not see into them without a flashlight. They did not have electricity or heat.

Solitary confinement cells could be found on the second floor. These had solid walls, no light and solid doors instead of steel bars. There was a large room that I was told was used to house women and juveniles. Here, it appears they slept on cots or the floor.

The brick façade of the old Alfred jail.

The warden's peephole in the wall allowed him to keep an eye on the cellblock.

Peeling paint on a cell door.

Eventually, this jail will be remodeled and fitted out with electricity and new businesses. The bars will be removed from the windows. A new jail now stands in Alfred. This old one was discontinued in 1940. Having toured this bleak old place, it is not so difficult to see what drove so many to attempt suicide here.

TWELVE O'CLOCK HIGH

On a quiet spring day in May 1943 in Kennebunk, the branches of the giant Lafayette elm shook and the water tower off High Street rattled with the echo of the sound of a low-flying bomber. Many startled residents, fearful of the possibility of attack during that early phase of World War II, thought that the enemy had come.

It was quickly learned that the plane that brushed the treetops that day had in fact been an American B-17 Flying Fortress. Residents also learned that the crewmember responsible was Leslie Nadeau, a Kennebunk native known to his friends as "Red" or "Gunk." On the nose of the plane was painted a lovely girl on a half moon and the words "High Life."

Nadeau and his crew were on their way to war, flying from the Midwest as part of the 100th Bombardment Group. Nadeau and the other members of the crew of their plane, named the *High Life* after a popular beer, were on their way first to Bangor, Maine, and then to Thorpe Abbots Airbase in England. En route, they decided to break from formation briefly to buzz Nadeau's hometown.

In France on June 25, they flew their first combat mission. Of the original thirty-five crews (ten men each) sent to England that day, twenty-seven were lost in combat by October. The 100th became known as "the Bloody Hundredth."

On the thirteenth bombing mission, the *High Life* became part of a historic air battle later recounted in Hollywood by the making of the film *Twelve o'Clock High* starring Gregory Peck. Not one of the crewmen knew when they awoke at 2:00 a.m. for their briefing that day that it would be their last mission.

Nadeau, small in stature, was the ball turret gunner. The target that day was the Messerschmitt fighter plane factory in Regensburg, Germany. After a long delay caused by local weather conditions, the mission was on. They assembled in their assigned tail-end position known as "coffin corner" behind a massive air armada that stretched four miles across England and included 160 Flying Fortresses.

By 10:00 a.m., enemy fighters in countless numbers swarmed in on them. A savage air battle followed. Flying on the right wing of the *High Life* that day was the B-17 of Lieutenant Colonel Beirne Lay. Lay, who later wrote the book *Twelve o'Clock High*, remembered at one point during the battle:

> *A shining object sailed past over our right wing, I recognized it as a main exit door. Seconds later a dark object came hurtling through our formation, barely missing several props. It was a man, clasping his knees to his head, revolving in a triple somersault. I didn't see his chute open.*

After constant attack for a solid hour, the *High Life* suffered severe damage and two engines failed. Unable to keep up with the rest of the squadron,

Leslie "Gunk" Nadeau and his wife, Evelyn, and a movie poster for *Twelve o'Clock High* starring Gregory Peck.

a decision was made to try to make a landing in neutral Switzerland. The pilot pulled away from the formation and started toward Switzerland, thirty minutes away. In the process of reaching Switzerland, they inadvertently flew directly over a German antiaircraft school. The *High Life* again took a beating but luckily escaped.

The *High Life* was the first plane of World War II to crash-land in Switzerland, much to the surprise of the farmer who owned the field in which the plane came to rest on its belly. The entire crew crawled out safely from the wreck and was immediately surrounded by Swiss soldiers. One soldier, who spoke impeccable English, told them, "For you, the war is over."

They remained interred in Switzerland until the Allied forces invaded France in 1944.

Nadeau then "jumped the fence into France" and found his way home. He requested another tour of duty in Sergeant Bluff, Iowa, where he married a woman named Evelyn Gallagher, a schoolteacher he had met there before being shipped out to England.

In 1983, forty years after that last flight, the Miller Brewing Company, inspired by the story of the crew whose plane was named after their beer, paid for a reunion of its members. All but two could attend. Gregory Peck, who was also invited but could not attend, sent a letter to the crew that read, in part:

> *I thank you, as members of the 100th Bomb Group, better known as the "Bloody Hundredth," for providing me with one of my most challenging film roles. It was an honor for me to portray General Savage in* 12 O'clock High, *the story of your thirteenth and last bombing mission, one of the most decisive missions of World War II. Your courage, determination and devotion to each other and to your country make you the kind of heroes that never go out of style.*

If you get a chance, try to see that old film *Twelve o'Clock High* because now you know "Gunk" Nedeau was there!

VISION OF MARS

In 2005, we began seeing images of Mars taken from the Odyssey spacecraft. These remarkable images were breathtaking. They did not, however, resemble those in our mind's eye, the ones humanity had fantasized about for over one hundred years. For years, we had been dreaming about what or who could be found on the Red Planet. Comic strips and early film and TV gave us *Flash Gordon, Buck Rogers, Lost in Space* and *Star Trek*. Now that was imagery!

I'd like to print a story written in 1910 by an unknown Kennebunk High School student. The story, entitled "A Letter from Mars," gives us a fictional idea of what one young man thought Mars would be like if we ever got there. The story takes the form of a letter home from Mars:

> *Planet Mars, July 25, 2000*
> *Dear Sister*
> *I presume the time has seemed to you long since I set upon my journey, but this is the first opportunity I have had of writing since our arrival and I should not have had this if two of our company had not become suddenly homesick. They have decided to return at once, so I thought this my only chance to mail you a letter.*

Buster Crabbe in an early movie poster for *Mars Attacks*.

On the fourth day something gave out in the air machine which compelled us to go much slower the remainder of the distance. We arrived safely at the end of the fifteenth day. We judge of the time by the amount of food we have consumed. Being thoroughly exhausted we stretched ourselves upon the cool velvety turf and sleep took possession of our weary frames.

When we awoke, the sun shone brightly. Words would fail to describe the weird and picturesque scenery which unfolded before my eyes as I sat up and gazed around me. It was just one vast panorama of beauty.

One of the greatest peculiarities of Mars is its vegetation which is a dark red color. This looked queerly to me at first, but I have become quite accustomed to it now, although I often long for a glimpse of green fields upon the dear old Earth again. The color of the soil is dark green and in places black.

There are some of the most beautiful lakes here that I ever saw. Just below our camp is a small one whose waters are deep pink. In some, the waters are purple, others yellow, blue, etc. We have traversed a considerable amount of the planet but have found no mountains yet. There are some of the grandest forests here that man can possibly conceive of. It is no uncommon sight to see a tree fifty feet in diameter. We are going to remodel one of these huge giants and make it suitable for habitation.

The evenings here are delightful. There are two moons, Dread and Terror that resemble two great balls of fire. Many of the stars look to be as large as the moon appears to us when viewed from Earth. On a clear night the stars can be seen continuously shooting in all directions, which gives the heavens the appearance of a vast system of fireworks.

We have long since come to the conclusion that there are no human beings besides ourselves on Mars. The morning following arrival I took my gun and went in search of dinner. But my heart failed me when an innocent deer looked into my face so fearless and happy. Partridges walked by my side, birds of rare plumage lit upon my shoulders and beautiful horses sniffed curiously at my hands. I returned to camp empty handed having come to the conclusion that I had rather subsist on "hardtack" and "Boston Baked Bean" than to kill those beautiful creatures.

Please have the following item inserted in the leading papers:

Mars is now ready for settlement. The grand old stars and stripes are already planted in the soil. It is desired that there be a large number of men from all trades and professions in the next trip for the colonization of the planet. Let all who will volunteer, apply to the board of examiners in Washington, D.C. Notice: Through trains with sleeper cars attached will be used on the next trip.

Your affectionate brother,

Harold

SLAVERY IN MAINE

A man by the name of Joseph Hill died in 1743. His estate listed three slaves named Sharper, Plato and Tom. By 1743, slavery had been practiced in New England for nearly a century.

In a report written in 1745, Wells was listed as having eleven slaves, and Kittery had forty-two. This deplorable trade was carried out in all of New England. In the town of York, at a building called the Weare Home, which no longer stands, slaves were bought and sold. Many prominent men mentioned in the histories of York County owned slaves.

Among these men were Waldo Emerson of Summer Street in Kennebunk. Colonel John Wheelwright of the Wells Garrison had slaves, as did John Bourne, who had a slave named Salem Bourne. John Hobbs of Kennebunkport owned two slaves named Zelph and Phillis. He sold the five-year-old daughter of Phillis to a man in Saco. The image is horrifying to imagine.

Thankfully, by the late 1700s, most slaves in New England were freed. At that time, eight families of freed slaves took up residence in the woods of Kennebunk. Just under a mile from the west bank of the Mousam River, on the left side of the road known as High Street, there is a trail leading into the forest. This forest is actually a memorial forest by deed, given to the State of Maine by descendants of the Bragdon family, who lived across the road. If you are to follow this trail into the woods for about two hundred feet, you will discover a long ridge of land crossing your path. This ridge, which shows clearly on topographic maps of the area, was in its day called Nigger Ridge. A hateful term to be sure, and one we are glad is gone from modern-day conversation. Here on this ridge dwelt a dozen or more freed slaves. Somewhere in this vicinity is their final resting place as well.

One of the freed men was named Tom. Later in life, he was called "Old Tom." According to the many wills and documents regarding slavery in Maine, Tom was among the few African Americans to have a recorded last name. His was Bassett. He lived on the ridge with fellow freed slaves Phillis, Chance, Sharper, Cato, Salem, Peg, Primus, Hannah and an Indian woman named Dinah.

They managed to scrape out an existence, perhaps by making brooms and baskets, raising vegetables and jobbing for persons in the neighboring villages. Phillis and Tom were originally owned by Captain James Littlefield of Wells and were married in 1776. Sharper and Hannah Simon married in 1744. When Old Tom was in his eighties, his wife, Phillis, died. He took up with another freed slave named Peg. Old Tom was known for being able to play the fiddle and was frequently asked to play at social functions in town. He died in 1831. He was believed to be at least one hundred years old at

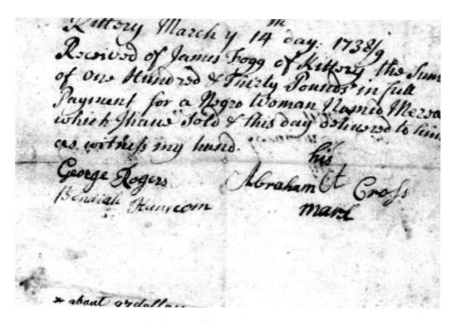

An early slave sale document. *Courtesy of the Maine Historical Society.*

the time. His funeral was attended by Reverend Wells. In Bourne's *History of Kennebunk*, it was said that the ladies in the neighborhood on the ridge were present but there were not enough men to convey his coffin to the grave without the aid of Reverend Wells. When and how the rest of the group passed away is not recorded.

I have walked the ridge many times over the years in hopes of finding evidence of their existence or perhaps evidence of their cemetery. I have located one fieldstone that may indicate that last resting place of these souls. Hopefully, modern expansion of home building in Kennebunk will never reach their place in these woods.

WITCH TROT LAND

Where is Witch Trot Land? There is an old book occasionally available in antiques stores or in online auctions that is called *Witch Trot Land*. It was published in 1937 by Anne Mountfort and Katherine Marshall. This neat little paperback publication contains historic details about York County, Maine, which is what they refer to as Witch Trot Land.

In their book, you will find information about the early settlements of Kittery, the Berwicks, Eliot, York, Ogunquit, Wells, Alfred and the Kennebunks. Also in this book, you will learn how these towns got their names and read stories of many of the earliest settlers. In the pages of *Witch Trot Land*, you can also read about some interesting legends of York County.

Because this book is fairly rare, I thought you would like to know some of the things that it reveals. Kittery, settled in 1623 or earlier, was the first to receive a charter from the Massachusetts Bay Colony in 1647 and at one time was visited by George Washington. Descriptions are given of the Pepperell Mansion, built in 1682, and the Bray House, which was reportedly built in 1662. Other descriptions are given of the Sparhawk House, Follett House and Star Island Lighthouse.

In Eliot, the first normal school in Maine, Eliot Academy, is said to have been built in 1839. Also in Eliot, at William Everett's Tavern, all Piscataqua citizens signed their submission to Massachusetts. Apparently, Maine's first law office was opened in Eliot in 1725.

The authors wrote of Saint Aspinquid, patron saint of York, who supposedly was an Algonquin Indian and preached among sixty-six different Indian tribes, as far away as the Great Lakes. At the age of one

The cover of the book
Witch Trot Land.

hundred, he returned to Mount Agamenticus and died. Legend has it that fourteen different tribes sent their sachems to his funeral, and more than six hundred wild animals were burned on his funeral pyre at the summit of the mountain.

Very little is told of Ogunquit except that it is said that this village took its name from a Natick Indian phrase that means "a beautiful place by the sea." As with most towns in York County, many definitions have been given for its name over the years.

A funny anecdote about Wells is related in the story of Reverend Joseph Smith, who went to Wells "with the avowed intent to overthrow the work of the Devil." Smith was a Free Will Baptist, and to him, the devil was the Congregational Church. He preached at and harangued the Congregational

Church and even put one shoulder under a corner of the building in an attempt to take it off its foundation. The only result was a lame shoulder.

Among the many definitions of the name "Kennebunk," this book offers an explanation that it is an Indian term that means "the place where he thanked him." I am not at all sure who "he" or "him" is in this context.

The tragic tale of the bark *Isadore* is recounted in the paragraphs written about Kennebunkport, with stories about the ominous dreams some of the sailors had prior to the ship's fatal voyage. Only seven crewmembers' bodies were found after the *Isadore* wrecked on rocks off Cape Neddick in 1842. Those seven were buried in Kennebunkport. The body of the ship's captain, Leander Foss, was never recovered.

Finally, and most intriguing to me, are the legends of the Berwicks. According to legend, in 1670, Congregationalist Parson Burroughs came to preach in various places throughout Maine. He finally settled in Wells. According to descriptions, he was short and stocky in stature, had sandy hair and was very strong. It was circulated that he would put his finger in the muzzle of a sixteen-pound, flintlock rifle and lift it straight up, at arm's length. It was also rumored that he could raise a full barrel of cider and drink directly from its spout. Eventually, the people from Wells and those from his former hometown of Salem, Massachusetts, came to believe that he was a witch. They believed his extraordinary strength must have come from the devil. Several men were sent to Wells to seize him and return him to Salem for trial. On their journey back to Salem through Berwick, the road was spooky and a storm was brewing. Thunder crashed, lightning flashed and the hooves of the men's horses appeared to not touch the ground as they walked. All were convinced that Burroughs had cast a spell on them. Following his trial in Salem, Reverend Burroughs was hanged. The road in Berwick over which they traveled is now called Witch Trot Road.

WILLIAM BARRY

Merchant William Lord built the building that now houses the Brick Store Museum on Main Street in Kennebunk in 1825. This building operated as a dry goods store for many years. His grandson was named William Barry and was born in 1846. Barry was a noted architect but is better known for his efforts as a historian.

THIS TABLET
MARKS THE SITE
OF THE
WHEELWRIGHT
GARRISON
BUILT IN 1642 OR 1643
BY
REV. JOHN WHEELWRIGHT
ALSO
THE END OF THE
KING'S HIGHWAY
KNOWN AS
TOWN'S END

The original Wheelwright
Garrison marker placed by
William Barry in Wells.

After completing his architectural studies in Boston, Barry returned to Kennebunk. Barry, also an artist, drew many sketches of local homes and landscapes. He was an avid mapmaker and drew many maps that highlighted historical aspects of Wells and Kennebunk. He was also an author who wrote both historical and architectural books.

He studied old documents and interviewed older residents to learn as much as he could of our colonial heritage. He restored a local tavern known as Jefferd's Tavern. He promoted Old Home Week celebrations and erected several monuments in the area commemorating historic events.

His granite monuments, eight feet tall with bronze inscriptions, were placed in locations at the site of the Wheelwright Garrison in Wells; the Larrabee Garrison in Kennebunk; the winter campsite in Biddeford Pool of Richard Vines, who came here in 1616; and Joseph Storer's Garrison in Wells. The

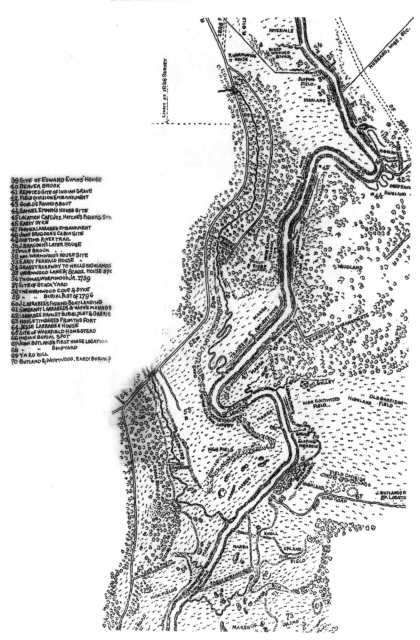

One of William Barry's many maps.

The marker that stands on private land just off the Bridal Path in Kennebunk marking the location of the Larrabee Garrison, which was the first settlement in Kennebunk.

monuments still stand; however, the one marking the Wheelwright Garrison was moved across Route 1 to the east side of the road a number of years ago.

The monument marking the location of the Larrabee Garrison is situated off what is called the Bridal Path in Kennebunk. It is on private property and can barely be seen now because of the forest growth around it. The Bridal Path is really the remains of an old railroad bed for a portion of railroad that was built between Kennebunk and Kennebunk Beach in the 1800s to accommodate the tourist industry. Barry placed this monument to mark the site where the first settlement of Kennebunk stood. Nearby are the graves of the original settlers, although their graves are no longer marked. Farther downriver along the Bridal Path is another pioneer cemetery of the early Wormwood and Butland families, who built the first ship on the Mousam River. Only a few scattered and broken stones remain there. These early settlers endured many hardships, including the Indian Wars of the mid-1700s. They were a stalwart breed.

Barry also had a talent for making models of historic homes. He painstakingly created miniature replicas of the Parson Home in Kennebunk, Jefferd's Tavern in Wells and many others. The majority of these are now found at the Brick Store Museum.

His personal collections of historical artifacts, writings, maps and drawings were the basis of the creation of the Brick Store Museum by his niece, Edith Barry. It is fitting that the museum occupies the building built by his grandfather in 1825. It serves as a legacy to a man who was fascinated with our colonial heritage.

THE KENNEBUNKPORT PLAYHOUSE

In the fall of 1971, a fire devastated the renowned Kennebunkport Playhouse. Arson was suspected, but no one was ever charged with the crime. The morning following the fire, a constant stream of cars passed the scene with saddened onlookers. This had been an icon of the community since the early 1930s.

Many folks remember the famous movie stars, politicians, singers and stage actors who came to Kennebunkport and surrounding towns each summer to attend the playhouse.

The playhouse was the brainchild of a man named Bob Currier who had graduated from the New England Conservatory and formed a repertory group in Newton, Massachusetts, called the Garrick Players.

During a summer visit to Kennebunkport, Bob met Booth Tarkington, who at the time was already a Broadway playwright and Pulitzer Prize winner. Tarkington was impressed with young Currier and became a sponsor of the Garrick Players. The Garrick Players began coming to the Olympian Club in Kennebunkport in 1929, according to Currier. But according to writer Patrice Tobin, who wrote a wonderful history of the playhouse in 1991, the very first performance of the Garrick Players was given on July 10, 1933. I'm not sure which date is correct, but the play in 1933 was a comedy called *Prince of Liars*. Patrons were charged thirty-five cents per seat and fifty cents if they reserved their seat.

Each year, the Garrick Players performed in the summer in Kennebunkport and in the winter in Newton, Massachusetts. By 1940, they were attracting New York critics, as well as some of the best-known stars of stage and screen.

An early postcard shows the first Garrick Players playhouse in Kennebunkport.

Motivated by his desire to have his own playhouse property, Bob purchased the old Merrill farm on the River Road, opposite the golf course. It had a barn that he hoped to convert into a playhouse. He worked diligently, alone and at times in freezing temperatures, to remodel the inside of that 150-year-old barn. By the summer of 1940, it had three hundred comfortable seats and an excellent view of the stage. It was also advertised as having plenty of parking and a cool breeze. It was considered better equipped than several playhouses then on Broadway. Currier provided shuttles to transport people from Kennebunk, Kennebunkport, Kennebunk Beach and Cape Arundel to his playhouse.

When America entered the Second World War, the playhouse closed. It remained closed for the length of the war. Bob enlisted in the air force and was assigned to Victorville Air Force Base in California. While there, he was responsible for providing the troops with quality entertainment. Following the war, the Kennebunkport Playhouse again opened its doors in the summer of 1946, presenting a comedy called *Blithe Spirit*. Booth Tarkington, who had passed away only weeks prior to the opening, was said to have been there in spirit as well.

The following summer, just four hours after the closing of the final performance, the barn became engulfed in flames. Rather than give up, Currier immediately rebuilt. He did so by first dismantling an old barn in Alfred, Maine. Each piece was numbered and then transported by truck to the site, where it was all reassembled. In the summer of 1950, the playhouse reopened on schedule. This larger structure measured seventy-six by forty feet and could seat 456 people. An additional thirty feet were added to the barn for a dressing room.

During the 1950s, the playhouse also hosted distinguished singers in musical productions. One favorite singer of the day was Bob's younger sister, Jane Morgan. Jane had established her singing career in Paris, Rome, London and other foreign cities. She first appeared in Kennebunkport with actor Russell Nype in Cole Porter's *Paris*. It was a complete sellout! After that, Jane would return each season for at least one performance. By this time, the company had ceased to use the name Garrick Players.

From 1937 until 1971, the playhouse presented over three hundred performances. Its roster of stars included Henry Morgan, Myrna Loy, Lillian Gish, Bette Davis, Tallulah Bankhead, Aaron Burr, Colleen Dewhurst and Gloria Swanson. Among its patrons were notables such as President Richard Nixon, Ruth Gordon and Helen Hayes. Local resident Kathryn Hussey told me that she lost her shoe during one of Hugh O'Brian's performances while she sat in the front row. She said that she received quite a scowl from the actor. Nelson Wentworth remembers working in Dock Square one summer at Mariners Clothing Store when a crowd of people began clamoring that Bette Davis was coming to town. Sure enough, the doors opened, and Nelson remembers Davis's purposeful walk as she made her way toward him. She told him that she needed to buy a pair of sneakers. To this day, he laughs at being able to say that he was lucky enough to touch the ankle of Bette Davis. I imagine that many others can recall a brush with celebrities during those years as well.

Bob Currier died in 1991. His sister Jane gave a tribute performance for him at the Sea Road School in Kennebunk that same year. Jane, Mrs. Jerry Weintraub (whose real name was Flossy Currier), resides in California during the winters and owns a farm on North Street in Kennebunkport called Blueberry Hill, which she visits during the summer.

THE SACO DRIVE-IN THEATRE

My dad had a strange sense of humor. For instance, we had a beagle; not a high-brow breed by any stretch, but my dad named her FiFi. Similarly, I had a boyfriend in junior high school named Bruce. Would my dad call him by his given name? Of course not! He called him Omar. Why? Well, I haven't

One of the last standing drive-in movie screens in Maine is located in Saco.

a clue, even to this day. We had a favorite restaurant named Chick's Diner, which my father never referred to as anything other than Quack's Place. These odd naming conventions applied even to the family car, which was a station wagon. That big, blue, steel, tail-finned road locomotive was called the Blue Goose.

I remember this because it was in that very same car that our family of four and the beagle named FiFi drove to the thriving metropolis of Binghamton, New York, to get to the drive-in theatre. The drive-in theatre played a big role in my childhood. We saw there the *Absent-Minded Professor* and *Herbie the Love Bug*, as well as scores of other movies. We would pile into the car with pajamas, pillows and popcorn and then head out as if on safari. I loved going, although I'm not sure that the beagle felt the same way.

My memory of that experience sparked my desire to share the same with my own daughters. I have been harboring the notion that drive-in theatre days are numbered. There are only five operating in Maine at this time. One is in Saco, Maine.

The entrance to the Saco Drive-In on Route 1.

The Saco Drive-In marquee.

The Saco Drive-In was built in 1939 and was originally called the Auto Drive-In. The name was changed in the 1950s. The original owner was Eugene Boragine. What a great ring to that name! Nowadays, it is owned and operated by Roberge Construction, Inc. It has a large field and holds five hundred cars. I was interested to discover that the speakers that they once used to clip onto car windows are no longer used. This is probably a good thing, as the Blue Goose accidentally tore more than its fair share off their mounts. What a clatter that made! Now, to hear the sound for the movie, you simply tune to the designated radio channel.

It was a delight to find that the concession stand at the Saco Drive-In was the same as all the concession stands of bygone days. Ice cream, popcorn, candy and soda could all be had at reasonable prices.

All in all, my daughters and I had a great time—a bit of nostalgia that is still available, inexpensive and entertaining. If you get a chance to go before the drive-ins become a thing of the past, don't forget to bring your pillows!

CAPTAIN JAMES FAIRFIELD

Today's leading industry in York County is tourism. Many who now come to visit our beaches and small towns are probably unaware of the shipping industry from which these towns sprang.

Every now and then I will come across a photo of an old sailing ship and wonder about the lives of the sailors and captains who sailed our waters in the eighteenth and nineteenth centuries. Their lives had to have been difficult. Some photos, paintings, letters and documents exist in our local libraries, historical societies and museums that give us a glimpse of the perils that these men faced.

There is one story in particular that I find fascinating. It is the story of a sea captain and a portrait of him that he sent home to his wife in 1806.

At the Brick Store Museum in Kennebunk there is a portrait, in oil, of a young man with dark hair who casts a steady gaze while holding a letter in his right hand. The portrait is of Captain James Fairfield, who at the time was only twenty-two years old. The letter he holds is clearly addressed to his employer, Tobias Lord of Kennebunk, Maine.

Like his father before him, Fairfield was given command of one of Tobias Lord's ships, and in 1806 he left his young wife to command the brig *Somers*.

His trading missions frequently took him to Charlestown, New Orleans, southwestern Europe and England.

On one such voyage, he decided to have his portrait painted. When it was finished, he had it rolled up and sealed inside a tin canister. He then sent the portrait home to his wife onboard another ship so that it would reach home before his own return. It never arrived. Fairfield was saddened to learn that the ship that he had chosen to carry it was lost at sea.

Fairfield's next command was aboard a two-masted ship named the *Macdonough* in 1812. No sooner was the ship away from Kennebunkport when all onboard were captured by a British frigate. As was customary during the War of 1812, he and his crew were taken to Dartmoor Prison in England and retained there for three long years. While there, he survived a

A sailing ship from the 1860s.

The portrait of Captain James Fairfield, recovered from the ocean.

massacre by prison guards in which eight prisoners were shot and forty-five others were wounded. None of these was from Kennebunk.

In December 1814, the Treaty of Ghent began to ensure prisoners' releases. Fearing that he would be unable to endure remaining in prison any longer, Fairfield bought another man's place on the first ship to take prisoners home. Unfortunately, when names were called to board the ship, the man to whom Fairfield had given his money took his own turn. In a letter home to his wife, Fairfield wrote, "I soon did expect to be free from this prison but our expectations have failed."

Eventually, he was released and returned to his Kennebunkport home. Sadly, just five years later he became ill and died shortly afterward at the early age of thirty-six. His wife died a short time later.

Two years after Fairfield's death, his former employer, Tobias Lord, was summoned to meet with the captain of a Swedish ship anchored in Portland Harbor. Tobias had heard of Fairfield's lost portrait years earlier and, like everyone else, assumed it to be resting on the ocean's floor. His amazement must have been immeasurable when the captain of the Swedish ship presented him with the portrait!

The address painted on the letter shown in the portrait had enabled the painting to be returned to its home port at last. Apparently, when the ship carrying the portrait sank, the tin case that held the canvas was buoyant enough to make its way to the surface of the ocean, where it managed to float for years and countless miles before being spotted by the Swedish vessel.

The painting was then taken to Captain Fairfield's sister, Polly, who, with her family, cherished it and its strange history for generations. The last family member to inherit it donated it to the Brick Store Museum.

IF TREES COULD TALK

I received an e-mail a while back from a fellow named Bill Bassett. Bill, a self-proclaimed "transplant from Vermont," has lived out on the Cole Road in Upper Alewive since 1996. He wanted to share an idea for a story with me.

He told me of an ancient tree out near the end of Cole Road in what is known as Clark's Pasture. I knew just the one he meant as I have admired and photographed this tree for years. I was glad to know that with the number of cars that fly down that road, someone else took notice and was curious about this particular tree.

The tree I am referring to is a giant oak that stands by the side of Cole Road just before the intersection with Walker Road. It has giant branches that lean to the ground and a circumference of seventeen and a half feet. As Bill wrote, "From the turn of the century, industrial revolution, numerous Nor Easters, World War I, World War II, fires of '47 and '57, this tree has survived." It's " full of bees in the summer" and has "branches the size of trees and a beauty shape."

Not being able to count its rings, I used a formula on the Internet for determining its age and found that it is approximately 165 years old. That would put the start of its growth at about 1839.

I imagine just who might have passed by this age-old tree in the years it has lived; no doubt, countless members of the Walker, Littlefield, Stone, Day and Cole families, to name only a few.

It has been cut back a few times to allow the phone lines to pass through the upper branches but still reaches gracefully across the road.

With the need for lumber over the years, I can only wonder why this tree survived. Something perhaps made it "special" to those who owned the land on which it grew. Perhaps it was a favorite meeting place or a beloved picnic

One of the oldest trees in Maine stands alongside the Cole Road in the Alewive District of Kennebunk.

spot. Maybe somewhere, twenty feet in the air, on one of those magnificent branches, are carved the initials of two lovers. It's hard to say, but I enjoy seeing it every time I drive down that road.

I'm glad to know others do as well. Thanks, Bill!

LABOR DAY REMEMBERED

The modern-day celebration of Labor Day grew out of the efforts of early labor unions that believed that there should be a workingmen's holiday to honor those who were responsible for building our nation. The first Labor Day celebration was held on Tuesday, September 5, 1882, in New York City.

The Central Labor Union adopted a Labor Day proposal and appointed a committee to plan a demonstration and picnic. They urged other organizations in other cities across the nation to hold similar celebrations.

A Labor Day parade in Kennebunk, Maine, circa 1897. *Courtesy of the Brick Store Museum.*

Eventually, in 1894, Congress passed an act making the first Monday in September of each year a legal holiday.

I purchased a letter several years ago that was written by a young lady named Grace Haley, who later married and became Grace Haley Burke. In it, Grace describes the 1897 Labor Day celebration. It does not indicate how old she was when she wrote the letter. I thought it would be fun to share her recollections from that long-ago Labor Day.

> *My Impressions of Labor Day 1897*
> *Labor Day was very pleasant but rather warm I thought. I got up very early and went out in the garden to get some flowers to trim my wheel. We had some lovely sweet peas and pansies. The parade was very fine. Some said it was much better than Old Orchard.*
>
> *One of the carriages was trimmed with orange and white and was very pretty. Two were trimmed with paper roses put all over the wheels and harness and another was white and green. It would be hard to say which was prettiest.*
>
> *The bicycles looked very nice, especially the two tandems. One of them was all flowers and the other red and white. Several of the wheels were red, white and blue. It was very hot riding as of course the wheels had no*

119

covering except the two tandems and as we had to get off every five minutes it was very tiresome.

After the parade came the hose race and the Safeguard won. In the afternoon the races were held and were very amusing. I was sorry the same man won in all the races.

The ball game occupied the last part of the afternoon but I did not go as I was very tired and did not want to. The concert in the evening was very fine and I enjoyed it. The fireworks were very pretty. I did not hear the speeches but I guess they were very good.

I was very tired when I got home but shall always remember Labor Day, 1897.
Grace Haley

What a lovely record of simpler times and happy memories. I hope your upcoming Labor Day celebrations are as relaxing as those of long ago!

OUR NATIVE AMERICAN HISTORY

A friend asked me which Native Americans lived in York County originally. I thought I would share some of the information I have read on the subject.

Artifacts have been found throughout our area that date back thousands of years to Paleo-Indians. Who are they, you ask? Simply put: prehistoric or ancient Indians. Some folks have been lucky enough to find arrowheads that date to these early Indians. The Paleo-Indians were nomadic and made temporary campsites.

Later, the Native Americans who inhabited our area at the time the English first came here were called the Abenaki tribe, which was part of the Algonquin nation. The Abenakis were not nomadic. The tribe was made up of a number of villages and had a ruler called a chief sachem. In Wells, that chief sachem of 1649 was known as Sagamore, or Chief Thomas Chabinocke. Interestingly enough, when the English first began settling Wells (of which Kennebunk was then a part) few Native American villages could be found because epidemics brought by earlier Europeans, such as smallpox, chickenpox and hepatitis, had come close to wiping them out. Originally, Wells was called Nampscoscoke and Ogunquit was called Negunquit. Kennebunk was called Kennebunk. The translation of these words varies

An Abenaki couple. *Eighteenth-century watercolor by an unknown artist.*

from source to source. I have read four or five different explanations for the source of the word "Kennebunk" alone.

Until the Pequot War of 1637 in the Connecticut Valley, the colonists and the Indians coexisted peacefully. Closer to home, King Philip's War of 1675 in and around Plymouth, Massachusetts, had far-reaching effects that set the tone for relations between the Native Americans and the European settlers. King Philip was actually an Indian chief of the Wampanoags and not an English ruler as some think. A variety of things led to these two wars, but the most predominant cause was the encroachment of English settlers on Indian land. Other wars followed. The term "Indian Wars" is a collective term used to describe the many wars that later followed.

During Queen Anne's War of 1702–13, forty-six residents of Wells were killed and twenty were captured. Among them were Mary Storer, Tabitha Littlefield and Esther Wheelwright. Esther was only seven years old when captured. She lived with the Indians for about five years before she was taken to Quebec. She eventually became a nun in Quebec, taking her vows in 1715. It is thought that Tabitha Littlefield remained with her Indian captors. A story circulated that many years later she returned briefly and identified herself to a local woman but did not remain. Mary Storer, also taken to Canada, decided to remain there and eventually married a Frenchman.

Peace between the Indians and the settlers finally came in 1760, only to be followed by more war, this time in the form of the American Revolution. It is interesting to note that many Native Americans fought in the American Revolution on the side of the Americans.

Wells historian Hope Shelley writes the following in her book, *My Name Is Wells—I Am the Town*:

> *Though it has been more than 300 years since the Abenaki Indians walked our shores, many reminders of them remain. Their Algonquian language is very much with us. Sachem, papoose, quahog, hominy, succotash and tomahawk are but a few that we recognize.*

For more information on the Abenaki tribe, one only has to enter the words "Abenaki Heritage" into any Internet search engine and hundreds of sites can be viewed.

REMEDIES AND AFFLICTIONS

Many times while reading old newspapers I come across unusual names of ailments and cures. Over time, I have come to realize just what they were referring to. I thought that I would share some of those old terms and their meanings.

In the 1800s, society was plagued by a disease called consumption. This disease continued to plague society until the 1940s, long after it took its current name of tuberculosis. For many years, all sorts of quack cures sprang up, including "Pectoral Balsam," "Seven Barks" and "Dr. Rhelf's Asthmatic Pills." Like many other quack cures of the day, these elixirs, ointments and pills claimed to cure a variety of other maladies as well. Dr. Rhelf's was also touted as a cure for ailments and complaints common to the female portion of society, such as hysterics, hypochondria, green sickness, sinking of the spirits, loathing of food and giddiness. This is easily explained when considering that

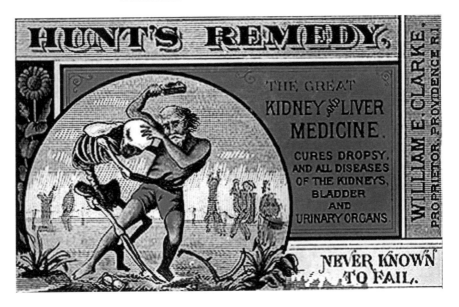

A label from an old quack medicine bottle.

many of the early medicines contained opium, heroin, morphine, mercury and other elements not then regulated by the government. For this reason, virtually anyone could create cure-all medicines.

Another sickness I find mentioned frequently in the 1800s is catarrh, which is what we now call a sinus infection. "Sick headaches" was the term used for migraine headaches that often cause nausea. "Dyspepsia" was the widely used term for upset stomach, and an "embrocation," from what I can tell, was the name given to a bruise or abrasion.

Still, there are many terms to which I cannot attach a modern equivalent. For instance, I have no idea what an illness called "St. Anthony's fire" was, nor "bilious colic," or what caused a "scald head."

I read with interest a cure for an affliction called phthisic. Someone with this ailment was told to put the skin of a weasel around his neck, with the hair facing outward, taking care not to apply it if the skin had dried out too much. I read recently that this disease is a wasting of the lungs similar to tuberculosis.

My grandmother, Ella, a farmer's wife, concocted her own homemade remedy known as "Oil-of-Tar." This foul-smelling, black oily liquid went on whatever ailed you. Lose a toenail? Oil-of-Tar. Fall on a pitchfork? Oil-of-Tar. No stitches, no doctor visits, just Oil-of-Tar. Recently, I learned that this remedy was a common homemade remedy used in rural areas as far away as the Appalachian Mountains and was made from the ash of a certain pine tree.

There were oils to prevent hair loss, oils to relieve sunburns and sarsaparilla to clear your complexion. Even the drink Moxie was thought to have curative powers. In the years prior to the Food and Drug Act of 1906, thousands of so called "patent" medicines were manufactured.

It seems to me that we've come a long way. Or have we? Don't you wonder about that hair product for men that is advertised on television and claims to cure baldness?

ODD SAYINGS AND THEIR ORIGINS

Have you ever heard someone say something that you've heard a thousand times and wondered how that saying came into existence? I think that most families have their own sayings. Some sayings can be found regionally and some even nationally. Here are a few and their meanings that I thought you would enjoy.

My cousin Renee e-mailed me the other day and said that she was "all in a dither" having to choose paint colors for her new home. Being from the dame ancestral gene pool, this is a familiar phrase to me. Where it got its original meaning was always a mystery. Now, with the advent of the Internet search engine, one can find the meaning for many of the sayings that have circulated for years. The word "dither" in fact originated in bombers during World War II. Small vibrating motors were used to reduce error in navigational computers. The movement they produced was referred to as dither. Modern dictionaries define dither as a highly nervous or agitated state.

One regional expression of course is "Down East." The popular magazine of the same name gives the following definition: "When ships sailed from Boston to ports in Maine, [which were east in direction] they were sailing with the wind at their backs, so they were sailing downwind. From this came the term 'Down East.'" It follows that when they returned to Boston, they were sailing upwind, and therefore many sailors referred to going "up to Boston," despite the fact that the city lies approximately fifty miles to the south of Maine's border.

Some of the more common sayings have colonial origins. For instance, the saying "being out of sorts" comes from the days of the early printing presses when trays of print type were used. The print letters were called sorts. If a printer ran out of sorts, he was left unable to finish the job.

The phrase "gone to pot" was also a colonial phrase. This referred to a candle whose wax remnants were too small to burn. These leftover bits were worthless unless returned to a pot over the fire and melted to form new candles.

"Mind your *p*'s and *q*'s" is a saying that has nothing to do with reading and writing. This saying originated when tavern keepers used to serve their ale in pints or quarts. When someone was drinking, he was advised to be mindful of how many pints and quarts (*p*'s and *q*'s) he drank.

The saying "mad as a hatter" does not come from *Alice in Wonderland*. Unfortunately, one of the main ingredients in making felt hats from colonial days was mercury. Persons employed in making hats often became disorientated, and some even became permanently impaired due to their exposure to this dangerous component.

The term "upper crust" originated in the early days of America when only the very best flour was used to make the top crust of pies to impress company. The bottom crust couldn't be seen, so it did not matter as much what type of flour went into it.

Some sayings like "two shakes of a lamb's tale" need little explanation; after all, have you ever seen how fast a lamb can shake its tale?

My family used quite a number of sayings while I was growing up. I'm told that they used more than was normal. Many are not suitable to print. Admittedly, we would not be considered an upper crust type of family. There is one saying of which I have never been able to determine the origins. When someone seemed a bit odd or out of the ordinary to my grandfather, he would say he or she was "odder than Dick's hat band." True to form, I will occasionally toss out this strange expression myself without thinking. Every time I do, whoever I am with will ask, "Just how odd is that and who is Dick anyway?" One day I may learn the true meaning of this phrase. Or perhaps it is better that I don't.

ABOUT THE AUTHOR

Kathleen Ostrander is the town historian of Kennebunk, an appointed position honoring her work to preserve local history. Her weekly column, "Paging through History," appeared in the *York County Coast Star* from 2002 to 2006. She is the archivist for the Kennebunk Free Library's Ken Joy Photographic Collection and formerly held a similar position with the Brick Store Museum, Kennebunk's main historical repository. Kathy has designed several exhibits for the museum and presents occasional lectures on area history. She is the author of Arcadia's *Kennebunk* and a member of the Kennebunk Art Guild. Kathy works as a Realtor© with Coldwell Banker Residential Brokerage and serves on the town's bicentennial committee.

Visit us at
www.historypress.net